Unlocking the Power of Derivatives

Alex Thompson

Published by Side Hustle Success, 2023.

UNLOCKING THE POWER OF DERIVATIVES

First edition. September 11, 2023.

ISBN: 979-8223966906

Written by Alex Thompson.

Table of Contents

To those who seek to understand the intricacies of financial derivatives, to the passionate learners and inquisitive minds, and to all who embark on the journey of financial mastery, this book is dedicated to you.

May you unlock the power of derivatives, navigate the complexities of the financial world, and find inspiration in the pursuit of knowledge and success.

With unwavering dedication to your financial journey,

Alex Thompson

Chapter 1: Introduction to Derivatives

In the opening chapter of our journey into the world of derivatives, we embark upon a fundamental exploration, setting the stage for a deeper understanding of these financial instruments.

Definition and Characteristics of Derivatives

Derivatives, as the name suggests, are financial instruments derived from other assets or underlying entities. They owe their existence to the fact that financial markets are not confined to just buying and selling stocks or bonds. They are a reflection of our need to manage risk, speculate on future prices, and optimize our financial strategies. Here, we delve into the core aspects of derivatives:

Definition of Derivatives

At its essence, a derivative is a contract between two parties, where the value is determined by changes in the price of an underlying asset or a related variable. These assets can include stocks, bonds, commodities, interest rates, and even cryptocurrencies. Derivatives essentially derive their value from something else, hence the name.

Let's break down this definition further. Imagine you're an investor interested in Apple Inc.'s stock. You anticipate that Apple's stock price will rise in the future, but you don't have enough capital to buy a significant number of Apple shares outright. Instead, you enter into a derivative contract known as a call option. This option gives you the right, but not the obligation, to buy Apple shares at a predetermined price (strike price) on or before a specified future date (expiration date). The value of this call option is directly tied to changes in Apple's stock price. If Apple's stock price increases, the value of your call option increases, allowing you to profit from the price rise without owning the actual shares.

Characteristics of Derivatives

Now, let's explore the key characteristics that define derivatives and make them such a dynamic and essential component of modern financial markets.

1. Leverage

One of the most prominent features of derivatives is their ability to magnify gains or losses. This concept of leverage is both a blessing and a potential curse for investors and traders. Leverage allows you to control a more substantial position with a relatively small amount of capital.

Consider the earlier example with the call option on Apple shares. If you bought 10 call options, each representing the right to purchase 100 Apple shares, you essentially control 1,000 shares of Apple stock. If Apple's stock price experiences a significant increase, your potential profit is multiplied compared to if you had invested the same amount directly in Apple shares.

However, it's crucial to recognize the flip side of leverage – it amplifies losses. If Apple's stock price moves against your expectations, the value of your call options can decline rapidly. In extreme cases, you could even lose your entire investment. This inherent risk of leverage underscores the importance of understanding derivatives thoroughly before using them and employing risk management strategies.

2. Speculation

Derivatives provide a playground for those who want to speculate on the future direction of prices. Traders can profit not only from rising markets (going long) but also from falling markets (going short). This dual nature of derivatives opens up a world of opportunities for traders with diverse market outlooks.

Let's extend our Apple call option example to illustrate speculation. If you believe that Apple's stock price will decline, you can enter into a put option contract. A put option gives you the right to sell Apple shares at a specified strike price on or before a predetermined expiration date. If Apple's stock price falls below the strike price, the put option becomes more valuable, allowing you to profit from the price drop. This ability to profit from both rising and falling markets is a hallmark of derivatives trading.

3. Risk Management

Beyond speculation, derivatives serve a vital role in managing risk. Hedgers use them to protect against adverse price movements in their core holdings. Consider a wheat farmer who is concerned about a potential drop in wheat prices at harvest time. To safeguard against this risk, the farmer can enter into a futures contract for wheat.

In a futures contract, two parties agree to buy or sell an underlying asset at a predetermined price on a specified future date. In this case, the farmer can sell wheat futures, ensuring a fixed selling price for their wheat crop when it's ready for market. If wheat prices fall, the futures contract offsets the financial loss incurred in the actual wheat sale. If prices rise, the farmer might miss out on potential profits in the cash market but is protected from the downside risk.

This risk management aspect of derivatives is invaluable in industries like agriculture, energy, and finance. It allows businesses and investors to hedge against unfavorable price movements, thereby providing stability and predictability in uncertain markets.

4. Variety

The world of derivatives is vast and varied, offering a spectrum of instruments tailored for specific needs and strategies. These instruments can be categorized into four primary types:

- **Options**: Options give the holder the right, but not the obligation, to buy (call option) or sell (put option) an underlying asset at a predetermined price within a specified time frame. They provide flexibility and can be used for both speculation and hedging.
- **Futures**: Futures contracts obligate the parties involved to buy or sell an underlying asset at a predetermined price on a specific future date. They are often used for hedging purposes and are prevalent in commodities markets.
- **Swaps**: Swaps are agreements where two parties exchange cash flows or financial instruments. Common types include interest rate swaps and currency swaps, which are used to manage interest rate and currency exchange rate risks, respectively.

- **Forwards**: Forwards are similar to futures but are typically customized contracts traded in the over-the-counter (OTC) market. They allow for more flexibility in terms of contract terms and specifications.

Each type of derivative serves a unique purpose and appeals to different market participants. Options are favored by traders seeking flexibility and leverage, while futures are popular among commodity producers and consumers looking to hedge price risk. Swaps and forwards, on the other hand, cater to specialized financial needs and are often tailored to suit specific circumstances.

5. Complexity

While derivatives offer powerful tools for managing risk and speculating on market movements, they can be complex and require a deep understanding of financial markets. This complexity has led to both tremendous success and catastrophic failures.

For instance, the global financial crisis of 2008 was exacerbated by complex derivatives called mortgage-backed securities (MBS) and credit default swaps (CDS). The intricate nature of these derivatives made it challenging for market participants and regulators to assess the associated risks accurately. When the housing market collapsed, the interconnectedness of these derivatives contributed to the widespread financial turmoil.

Therefore, it's imperative for anyone considering involvement in derivatives markets, whether as an investor, trader, or risk manager, to invest time in education and risk management. Understanding the intricacies, risks, and potential rewards of derivatives is paramount to making informed decisions and navigating these financial instruments effectively.

We'll uncover real-world examples and case studies to illustrate how derivatives are used in practice. So, buckle up as we navigate the exciting and, at times, tumultuous terrain of derivatives trading and investing, with the knowledge and insight to thrive in this dynamic financial landscape.

Historical Evolution of Derivatives Markets

The fascinating journey of derivatives markets through history is a testament to humanity's ingenuity in managing risk and adapting financial tools to evolving economic needs.

Ancient Beginnings

The concept of derivatives, in various forms, can be traced back to ancient civilizations. One of the earliest recorded instances of derivatives-like contracts dates back to ancient Mesopotamia, around 1754 BC. These ancient agreements involved promises of future payments for the delivery of specific goods, akin to what we now know as forward contracts. They allowed parties to secure prices in advance, thereby managing the risk of fluctuating commodity prices.

Medieval Europe and the Emergence of Futures Contracts

Moving forward in history, we find derivatives making their presence felt in medieval Europe. During the 17th century, Dutch merchants used tulip futures contracts, often regarded as one of the earliest examples of speculative trading in derivatives. These contracts allowed traders to speculate on the prices of tulip bulbs, which had experienced a speculative bubble.

The need for risk management in agriculture also gave rise to the development of futures contracts during this period. Farmers and merchants sought ways to guarantee prices for agricultural products in advance. These early futures contracts laid the groundwork for modern derivatives markets, as they introduced the concept of standardized contracts, where parties agreed to buy or sell an underlying asset at a predetermined future date and price.

The Birth of Modern Derivatives Markets

The 19th and early 20th centuries witnessed the formalization of derivatives trading in financial centers such as Chicago, where commodities like grains were actively traded. This period saw the establishment of futures exchanges, where standardized contracts for commodities were traded, leading to increased liquidity and transparency.

The Chicago Board of Trade (CBOT), founded in 1848, played a pivotal role in this development. It introduced standardized futures contracts for agricultural products, providing a platform for hedgers and speculators alike. This marked a significant step toward the modern derivatives markets we know today.

Options and Financial Innovation

While futures contracts thrived in the agricultural sector, options contracts were also evolving. Options had been traded informally for centuries, but it wasn't until the 20th century that formal options exchanges began to emerge.

The Chicago Board Options Exchange (CBOE), founded in 1973, is considered the birthplace of standardized options trading. The CBOE introduced listed options on individual stocks, allowing investors to hedge and speculate on stock price movements.

Financial innovation didn't stop there. The late 20th century witnessed the development of complex derivatives, such as interest rate swaps and credit default swaps (CDS). These instruments enabled financial institutions to manage their exposure to interest rate and credit risk, but their complexity also played a role in the 2008 financial crisis.

Regulation and Risk Management

As derivatives markets expanded and became increasingly sophisticated, the need for regulation and risk management became apparent. The Commodity Futures Trading Commission (CFTC) and the Securities and Exchange Commission (SEC) in the United States, along with other regulatory bodies globally, began implementing rules and oversight to ensure market integrity and stability.

Derivatives also gained prominence in risk management within the corporate world. Multinational corporations used currency derivatives to hedge against foreign exchange risk, and energy companies employed derivatives to manage exposure to volatile commodity prices.

The 21st Century and Beyond

In the 21st century, derivatives markets continued to evolve, with innovations like cryptocurrency derivatives entering the scene. The rise of digital assets brought about new opportunities and challenges, as markets grappled with the complexities of trading and settling digital derivatives.

Today, derivatives markets are integral to global finance, providing tools for investors, traders, and corporations to manage risk and optimize their financial strategies. While they offer immense potential, derivatives also carry risks, as highlighted by events like the 2008 financial crisis.

Understanding the historical evolution of derivatives markets helps us appreciate the journey of these financial instruments and the importance of responsible usage and regulation. In the chapters that follow, we'll delve deeper into the mechanics of various derivatives, their applications, and the intricacies of trading and risk management in modern derivatives markets. Join us as we navigate this fascinating world of finance.

Types of Derivatives: Forwards, Futures, Options, Swaps

In our exploration of derivatives, we've laid the foundation by defining what derivatives are and examining their historical evolution. Now, it's time to dive deeper into the diverse world of derivatives by exploring the four primary types: forwards, futures, options, and swaps. These derivative instruments serve distinct purposes and cater to a wide range of financial needs and strategies.

Forwards

Forward contracts are among the oldest forms of derivatives, with roots dating back to ancient civilizations. A forward contract is a customized agreement between two parties to buy or sell an underlying asset at a predetermined price on a specific future date. These contracts are typically traded in the over-the-counter (OTC) market, allowing for flexibility in terms of contract terms and specifications.

Forwards are often used for hedging purposes. Consider a scenario where a farmer plans to sell a harvest of wheat in six months. To lock in a price and protect against potential price declines, the farmer can enter into a wheat forward contract with a buyer. This ensures a fixed selling price for the wheat at the time of delivery, providing stability in an uncertain market.

However, forwards come with some limitations. They carry counterparty risk since they are customized contracts, and the parties involved must rely on each other to fulfill their obligations. Additionally, forwards lack liquidity compared to exchange-traded derivatives like futures.

Futures

Futures contracts share similarities with forwards but differ in several crucial aspects. Futures contracts are standardized agreements traded on organized futures exchanges. These standardized contracts feature predefined terms, including contract size, expiration date, and delivery procedures.

One of the primary advantages of futures contracts is their liquidity. Being exchange-traded, futures contracts can be bought or sold at any time before expiration, providing a high level of market liquidity. This liquidity attracts a diverse range of market participants, from speculators seeking profit opportunities to hedgers looking to manage risk.

For example, if an airline anticipates the need to purchase jet fuel in six months, they can use crude oil futures contracts to lock in a future price for the fuel. This hedges against potential price increases, providing cost predictability.

Options

Options contracts offer a different dimension to derivatives trading. Options provide the holder with the right, but not the obligation, to buy (call option) or sell (put option) an underlying asset at a predetermined price within a specified time frame. Options are versatile and can be used for various purposes, including speculation, hedging, and income generation.

For instance, consider an investor who owns shares of a technology company but is concerned about a potential downturn in the stock market. They can buy put options on their stock holdings. If the market declines, the put options increase in value, offsetting losses in the stock portfolio.

Options also come in different styles, such as American and European options, each with its exercise rules. American options can be exercised at any time before or on the expiration date, while European options can only be exercised at expiration.

Swaps

Swaps are derivatives that involve the exchange of cash flows or financial instruments between two parties. Swaps are highly customizable and serve various purposes, including managing interest rate risk, currency exchange rate risk, and credit risk.

One of the most common types of swaps is the *interest rate swap*. In this arrangement, two parties agree to exchange fixed and floating interest rate payments. This allows one party to hedge against interest rate fluctuations while the other seeks to benefit from changing interest rates.

Another significant type is the *currency swap*, where two parties exchange principal amounts and interest payments denominated in different currencies. This enables businesses with international operations to manage currency risk.

Swaps offer flexibility but also carry counterparty risk, as the parties involved rely on each other to fulfill their obligations.

Understanding these four primary types of derivatives—Forwards, Futures, Options, and Swaps—provides a solid foundation for navigating the world of financial derivatives. Join us as we continue our journey into the intricacies of derivatives trading and investing.

Market Participants and Their Roles

As we delve deeper into the world of derivatives, we not only examine the types and historical evolution but also explore the diverse array of market participants who play pivotal roles in the derivatives market. Understanding the different players and their functions is essential for gaining insight into how derivatives are utilized and how they impact the broader financial landscape.

1. Hedgers

Hedgers are market participants who primarily use derivatives to manage risk. Their goal is to protect themselves against adverse price movements in the underlying asset. Hedgers include:

- **Producers**: These are individuals or businesses that deal with the physical commodity or asset. For example, a farmer may use derivatives to hedge against the risk of falling crop prices.
- **Consumers**: Businesses that rely on the commodity or asset for their operations can also be hedgers. An airline might use derivatives to hedge against rising fuel prices.
- **Portfolio Managers**: Professionals managing investment portfolios may use derivatives to hedge against potential losses. For instance, a portfolio manager might use index futures to protect a portfolio from a broad market decline.

Hedgers use derivatives to minimize price uncertainty, ensuring more predictable outcomes for their businesses or investments.

2. Speculators

Speculators are participants who actively seek profit opportunities in the derivatives market by betting on the direction of price movements. They do not have an underlying exposure to the asset but instead take positions based on their market outlook. Speculators include:

- **Individual Traders**: These are retail investors who engage in derivatives trading for personal gain. They may trade futures or options on various assets based on their market analysis.
- **Institutional Traders**: Hedge funds, proprietary trading firms, and other institutional investors often engage in speculative trading strategies using derivatives. They have the resources and expertise to make large-scale bets on market movements.

Speculators provide liquidity to the derivatives market, facilitating price discovery and ensuring that hedgers can easily enter and exit positions.

3. Market Makers

Market makers are financial institutions or individuals that specialize in facilitating trading by providing liquidity. They quote both buy and sell prices for derivatives contracts, creating a market for participants to trade against. Market makers profit from the spread—the difference between the bid and ask prices.

Market makers play a crucial role in ensuring that derivatives markets function smoothly and efficiently. They reduce transaction costs, minimize bid-ask spreads, and enhance market liquidity.

4. Arbitrageurs

Arbitrageurs are participants who exploit price discrepancies between related assets or markets. They engage in arbitrage to profit from market inefficiencies. Arbitrageurs ensure that prices across different markets remain in sync, preventing opportunities for riskless profit.

For example, if a futures contract on a stock index is trading at a significantly different price from the actual value of the underlying index, an arbitrageur may buy the futures contract while simultaneously selling the underlying index to capture the price difference.

5. Clearinghouses

Clearinghouses are vital entities in the derivatives market that act as intermediaries between buyers and sellers. They ensure the integrity of trades, guarantee contract performance, and mitigate counterparty risk.

When two parties enter into a derivatives contract, the clearinghouse becomes the counterparty to both sides of the trade. This arrangement eliminates the need for traders to worry about the creditworthiness of their counterparties. Clearinghouses collect margin from traders to cover potential losses, and they mark-to-market positions daily to settle gains and losses.

6. Regulators and Exchanges

Regulators and exchanges are entities responsible for overseeing and regulating derivatives markets. They establish rules and regulations to maintain market integrity, protect investors, and prevent market manipulation. Examples of regulators include the Commodity Futures Trading Commission (CFTC) and the Securities and Exchange Commission (SEC) in the United States.

Derivatives are typically traded on organized exchanges, such as the Chicago Mercantile Exchange (CME) or the Chicago Board Options Exchange (CBOE). These exchanges provide a centralized marketplace for participants to trade standardized contracts.

Regulatory Framework and Oversight

As we deepen our understanding of derivatives, it is crucial to explore the regulatory framework and oversight mechanisms that govern these financial instruments. The derivatives market, with its complexity and potential for risk, operates within a structured environment designed to ensure market integrity, protect investors, and maintain stability.

1. Regulatory Bodies

In the United States, the derivatives market falls under the jurisdiction of the *Commodity Futures Trading Commission (CFTC)* and the *Securities and Exchange Commission (SEC)*. These agencies have distinct responsibilities:

- *CFTC*: The CFTC primarily regulates derivatives contracts related to commodities, including futures and options on agricultural products, energy, and metals. It focuses on ensuring fair trading practices, market transparency, and preventing fraud and manipulation in commodity markets.
- *SEC*: The SEC oversees securities markets and certain derivatives tied to securities. It regulates options on individual stocks and some complex derivatives instruments, such as securities-based swaps.

Outside the United States, other regulatory bodies, such as the *Financial Conduct Authority (FCA) in the UK* and the *European Securities and Markets*

Authority (ESMA) in the EU, play similar roles in overseeing derivatives markets within their jurisdictions.

2. Market Oversight

Derivatives markets operate on organized exchanges and over-the-counter (OTC) platforms. Each type of market has its oversight mechanisms:

- *Exchange-Traded Derivatives*: Organized exchanges, like the Chicago Mercantile Exchange (CME) or Eurex, provide a regulated trading environment. These exchanges establish and enforce trading rules, monitor market activity, and ensure that contracts adhere to standardized specifications. Regulatory agencies oversee the exchanges to ensure fair and transparent trading.
- *Over-the-Counter (OTC) Derivatives*: OTC derivatives, customized contracts negotiated directly between two parties, present unique regulatory challenges. To address these challenges and mitigate counterparty risk, central clearinghouses have emerged. Clearinghouses, such as the Intercontinental Exchange (ICE) Clear or LCH.Clearnet, act as intermediaries, becoming the counterparty to both sides of a trade. They require participants to post margin and manage the settlement of contracts. This structure enhances transparency and reduces counterparty risk in OTC markets.

3. Reporting and Transparency

Regulatory oversight extends to reporting and transparency requirements. Participants in derivatives markets are typically required to report their trades and positions to regulatory authorities. This reporting serves several purposes:

- **Market Surveillance**: Regulators use trade data to monitor market activity, detect unusual trading patterns, and investigate potential market manipulation or abuse.
- **Risk Assessment**: By having access to comprehensive data, regulators can assess the level of risk in the derivatives market. This information

helps them identify systemic risks and take appropriate actions to maintain market stability.

- **Transparency**: Transparency is a critical component of market integrity. It ensures that market participants have access to accurate and timely information, fostering confidence in the market.

4. Dodd-Frank Act

In the wake of the 2008 financial crisis, the United States introduced significant regulatory reforms through the *Dodd-Frank Wall Street Reform and Consumer Protection Act* (Dodd-Frank Act). This legislation aimed to enhance transparency, reduce systemic risk, and improve the regulation of derivatives markets.

Key provisions of the Dodd-Frank Act included the introduction of mandatory central clearing for standardized OTC derivatives, increased reporting and recordkeeping requirements, and the establishment of the Volcker Rule to limit proprietary trading by banks.

5. International Cooperation

Derivatives markets are global in nature, and regulatory authorities recognize the importance of international cooperation. Regulatory bodies collaborate through forums such as the International Organization of Securities Commissions (IOSCO) and the Financial Stability Board (FSB) to harmonize regulations, address cross-border issues, and promote consistent oversight across jurisdictions.

Understanding the regulatory framework and oversight mechanisms is essential for participants in derivatives markets. Compliance with these regulations ensures market stability and safeguards the interests of investors.

Chapter 2: Forwards and Futures Contracts

Understanding Forwards Contracts

Forwards contracts, in particular, offer a fascinating glimpse into the world of customized, over-the-counter (OTC) derivative instruments.

What is a Forwards Contract?

A *forwards contract* is a legally binding agreement between two parties to buy or sell an underlying asset at a predetermined price (the *strike price*) on a specified future date (the *expiration date*). Unlike standardized futures contracts, forwards are highly customizable, allowing the parties involved to tailor the contract terms to their specific needs.

Key Components of a Forwards Contract

1. **Underlying Asset**: Every forwards contract revolves around an underlying asset. This can be almost anything – from commodities like oil, wheat, or gold to financial instruments such as currencies, bonds, or even stock indices.
2. **Strike Price**: The strike price, also known as the forward price, is the price at which the parties agree to buy or sell the underlying asset at the contract's expiration date. It reflects the anticipated future market value of the asset.
3. **Expiration Date**: The expiration date signifies when the parties are obligated to fulfill the terms of the contract. It's the point in the future when the actual exchange of the underlying asset and payment occurs.
4. **Quantity of the Underlying Asset**: The parties specify the quantity or volume of the underlying asset to be exchanged. It can vary widely, depending on the asset and the needs of the parties involved.
5. **Counterparty**: Forwards contracts are bilateral agreements, meaning they involve two parties – a buyer and a seller. The buyer agrees to purchase the asset at the specified price, while the seller commits to sell it.

Customization and Flexibility

The hallmark of forwards contracts is their flexibility and customization. Unlike standardized futures contracts, which are traded on organized exchanges with set contract specifications, forwards allow parties to negotiate and agree upon the contract terms individually. This flexibility is advantageous for hedgers and businesses with specific needs that may not align with standardized contracts.

Hedging with Forwards

One of the primary uses of forwards contracts is *hedging*. Hedging involves using derivatives to offset potential losses in the value of an underlying asset. Consider a multinational corporation that operates in multiple countries and is concerned about fluctuations in exchange rates. To protect itself from unfavorable currency movements, the corporation can enter into a forwards contract to lock in a future exchange rate for a specific currency pair.

For example, if a U.S.-based company anticipates receiving a large payment in euros six months from now, they can use a forwards contract to hedge against the risk of the euro weakening against the U.S. dollar. By agreeing to exchange a predetermined amount of euros for dollars at a specified future rate, the company secures the value of their expected payment, reducing uncertainty.

Speculation with Forwards

While hedging is a fundamental use of forwards, these contracts also provide opportunities for *speculation*. Speculators, who seek to profit from price movements, can take positions in forwards contracts based on their market outlook.

For instance, if an investor believes that the price of crude oil will rise in the coming months, they can enter into a long (buy) forwards contract for oil. If their prediction is correct and the oil price increases, they can sell the contract at a profit. Conversely, if the price falls, they may incur losses.

Risks and Considerations

Forwards contracts offer valuable risk management and speculative opportunities, but they are not without risks:

- **Counterparty Risk**: Since forwards are bilateral agreements, the parties involved are exposed to counterparty risk. If one party fails to fulfill their obligations, the other may face losses.
- **Lack of Liquidity**: Forwards are typically traded in the OTC market, which can lack the liquidity of exchange-traded derivatives. This may limit the ease of entering or exiting positions.
- **Customization Complexity**: While customization is a strength, it can also lead to complexity and negotiation challenges, particularly in complex or illiquid markets.

As we venture further into the world of derivatives, we'll explore how forwards contracts compare to standardized futures contracts, their mechanics, and their applications in various industries. Join us on this journey as we continue to unravel the intricacies of derivatives trading and investing.

Pricing Forwards Contracts

Understanding how these customized financial instruments are valued is essential for participants in the derivatives market, whether they are hedgers, speculators, or investors seeking to optimize their financial strategies.

The Time Value of Money

At the core of pricing forwards contracts is the concept of the time value of money. This fundamental financial principle recognizes that a sum of money today is worth more than the same sum in the future. In the context of forwards contracts, this means that the agreed-upon price (the strike price) for the underlying asset should account for the opportunity cost of not having that money available for investment during the contract's duration.

Pricing Formula for Forwards Contracts

The pricing of forwards contracts is straightforward and relies on two primary components:

1. **Spot Price (S)**: The spot price is the current market price of the underlying asset. It represents the asset's value today, without considering any future interest or dividends.
2. **Risk-Free Interest Rate (r)**: The risk-free interest rate is a critical determinant in pricing forwards. It reflects the potential return an investor could earn on a risk-free investment during the life of the forwards contract. Common benchmarks for the risk-free rate include government bond yields or the interest rate on short-term investments.

The formula for pricing a forwards contract is as follows:

F = Se^(rT)

Where:

- **F** represents the theoretical forward price.
- **S** is the current spot price of the underlying asset.
- **e** denotes the base of the natural logarithm (approximately equal to 2.71828).
- **r** is the risk-free interest rate.
- **T** represents the time to expiration of the forwards contract, measured in years.

This formula calculates the expected future price of the underlying asset at the contract's expiration, taking into account the opportunity cost associated with tying up capital in the forwards contract.

Understanding Forward Pricing

Let's illustrate forward pricing with a practical example:

Imagine a financial institution that enters into a one-year forwards contract to purchase 1,000 barrels of crude oil at a strike price of $70 per barrel. The current spot price of crude oil is $65 per barrel, and the prevailing risk-free interest rate is 5%.

Using the pricing formula, we can calculate the theoretical forward price (F):

F = $65 * e^(0.05 * 1)

F ≈ $68.22 per barrel

In this example, the theoretical forward price for crude oil is approximately $68.22 per barrel. This means that, according to the time value of money principle, the financial institution is willing to pay $68.22 today for the right to purchase crude oil at $70 per barrel in one year.

Factors Affecting Forward Prices

Several factors can influence the pricing of forwards contracts:

1. **Spot Price Movements**: Changes in the spot price of the underlying asset directly impact the forward price. A rising spot price typically results in a higher forward price, while a falling spot price leads to a lower forward price.
2. **Interest Rate Fluctuations**: Alterations in risk-free interest rates can significantly impact forward prices. Higher interest rates tend to increase forward prices, as they raise the opportunity cost of tying up capital.
3. **Dividends and Income**: For assets that generate income, such as dividend-paying stocks, the forward price may be adjusted to account for the expected income during the contract's duration.
4. **Carrying Costs**: In some cases, assets may incur carrying costs, such as storage and financing expenses. These costs can affect the forward price.
5. **Market Expectations**: Market sentiment and expectations about future price movements can also influence forward pricing. Traders and investors may adjust forward prices based on their outlook for the underlying asset.

Understanding these factors and their impact on forward pricing is crucial for making informed decisions in the derivatives market. Whether you are a hedger seeking to lock in prices, a speculator aiming to profit from market movements, or an investor looking to manage risk, a solid grasp of forward pricing is a valuable asset in your derivatives toolkit.

Uses and Applications of Forwards

Forwards contracts, with their flexibility and customization, find a wide range of uses and applications in various industries. In this section, we'll explore some of the primary ways in which forwards are employed by market participants, from hedging against price volatility to optimizing investment strategies.

1. Hedging Against Price Volatility

Hedging is one of the most common and essential applications of forwards contracts. Hedgers use forwards to protect themselves against adverse price movements in the underlying asset. This risk management strategy is particularly valuable for businesses exposed to volatile commodity prices, currencies, or interest rates.

For example, an airline company that anticipates needing a substantial amount of jet fuel in six months can enter into a forwards contract to purchase the fuel at a predetermined price. This hedges against the risk of rising fuel prices, ensuring cost predictability and protecting the company's profit margins.

2. Locking in Future Prices

Forwards contracts allow parties to lock in prices for future transactions. This is beneficial for both buyers and sellers, as it provides price certainty in an uncertain market environment.

- **Agricultural Producers**: Farmers frequently use forwards contracts to lock in prices for their crops or livestock. This shields them from the fluctuating prices in the agricultural commodities market.
- **Importers and Exporters**: Businesses engaged in international trade use currency forwards to secure exchange rates for future transactions. Importers can lock in favorable rates for their foreign currency payments, while exporters can protect themselves from unfavorable currency movements.

3. Speculation and Profit Generation

Speculators, who aim to profit from price movements in the underlying asset, also utilize forwards contracts. Unlike hedgers, speculators do not have an underlying exposure to the asset. They take positions in forwards based on their market outlook.

For instance, a speculator who believes that the price of a particular commodity will rise in the future can enter into a long (buy) forwards contract for that commodity. If the price indeed increases, the speculator can sell the contract at a profit. Conversely, if the price falls, they may incur losses.

4. Asset Allocation and Investment Strategies

Investors often incorporate forwards contracts into their asset allocation and investment strategies. They may use forwards to fine-tune their portfolio risk and returns. Some common applications include:

- **Portfolio Protection**: Investors concerned about potential market declines can use equity index forwards to protect their portfolio's value. If the market falls, the gains on the forwards contract can offset losses in the portfolio.
- **Income Generation**: Forwards can be used to enhance income generation. For instance, an investor can enter into a covered call forwards strategy, where they simultaneously hold a long position in an asset and sell a call option on that asset. This generates income through the option premium while potentially capping the upside potential.

5. Arbitrage Opportunities

Arbitrageurs actively seek opportunities to profit from price discrepancies between related assets or markets. Forwards contracts can be involved in various arbitrage strategies, helping to align prices and correct market inefficiencies.

For example, if an arbitrageur observes that the price of an asset in the spot market is significantly lower than the theoretically calculated forward price, they can buy the asset in the spot market and simultaneously sell a forwards contract on the same asset. This strategy aims to capture the price difference between the spot and forward markets.

6. Customized Risk Management

In addition to standardized risk management, forwards contracts offer highly customized risk solutions. Businesses and institutions with unique risk profiles and requirements can tailor forwards contracts to address specific challenges.

For instance, a company might use a customized forwards contract to hedge against a specific interest rate scenario that is not adequately covered by standardized derivatives.

Futures Contracts: Structure and Mechanics

In this section, we'll shift our focus from forwards to futures contracts, exploring their structure and mechanics. Futures contracts, unlike forwards, are standardized financial instruments traded on organized exchanges. Their uniformity and transparency make them a crucial component of global derivatives markets.

Structure of Futures Contracts

1. Standardization: One of the defining characteristics of futures contracts is their standardization. Unlike forwards, where contract terms are individually negotiated, futures contracts have predetermined specifications. These specifications include the underlying asset, contract size, expiration date, and delivery location. For example, a standard gold futures contract may specify the delivery of 100 troy ounces of gold with delivery in New York.

2. Clearinghouse Involvement: In futures markets, a clearinghouse acts as an intermediary between buyers and sellers. When two parties enter into a futures contract, the clearinghouse becomes the counterparty to both sides of the trade. This arrangement eliminates counterparty risk, as traders no longer need to rely on the financial stability of their counterparts. The clearinghouse also manages margin requirements and daily settlement of gains and losses.

3. Exchange-Traded: Futures contracts are traded on organized exchanges, providing a centralized marketplace for participants. Some well-known futures exchanges include the Chicago Mercantile Exchange (CME), the Intercontinental Exchange (ICE), and Eurex. These exchanges establish and enforce trading rules, monitor market activity, and ensure that contracts adhere to standardized specifications.

4. Mark-to-Market: One of the unique features of futures contracts is daily *mark-to-market* settlement. At the end of each trading day, the clearinghouse calculates the gains or losses for each trader based on the difference between the contract's settlement price and the previous day's settlement price. These gains or losses are then settled in cash. This mechanism ensures that traders have the necessary funds to cover potential losses and maintains market integrity.

5. Delivery and Settlement: While futures contracts can be physically settled by the delivery of the underlying asset, the majority of futures contracts are cash-settled. In cash-settled contracts, traders do not exchange physical assets but settle the contract's gains or losses in cash. The cash settlement amount is determined based on the difference between the contract's settlement price and the contract's initial price.

Mechanics of Trading Futures Contracts

The mechanics of trading futures contracts follow a structured process:

1. **Contract Selection**: Traders choose a specific futures contract based on their market outlook and objectives. They consider factors such as the underlying asset, contract size, and expiration date.
2. **Placing Orders**: Traders can place different types of orders, including market orders, limit orders, and stop orders. Market orders are executed immediately at the prevailing market price, while limit orders specify a maximum price (for buyers) or minimum price (for sellers) at which they are willing to trade.
3. **Execution**: When a buyer and seller agree on the terms of a futures

contract, the trade is executed on the exchange.

4. **Daily Settlement**: At the end of each trading day, the clearinghouse calculates gains or losses for each trader, which are settled in cash.
5. **Expiration and Delivery**: For physically settled contracts, traders who hold positions until expiration may be required to deliver or take delivery of the underlying asset. However, most contracts are cash-settled.

Leverage and Margin

One of the unique aspects of futures trading is the use of *leverage*. Traders are required to deposit a relatively small amount of capital known as *margin* to control a much larger position in the futures contract. Leverage magnifies both potential gains and losses. While leverage can enhance profit potential, it also increases risk, making proper risk management essential in futures trading.

In the following sections, we will further explore the advantages and disadvantages of futures contracts, their uses in various industries, and practical strategies for trading them. Join us as we continue our journey into the intricate world of derivatives trading and investing, with a focus on standardized futures contracts.

Margin Requirements and Clearing in Futures Markets

In the world of futures contracts, margin requirements and the role of clearinghouses play a vital role in maintaining market integrity and stability. In this section, we will delve into the concepts of margin, initial margin, maintenance margin, and how clearinghouses manage risk in futures trading.

Margin Requirements

1. Initial Margin: When traders initiate a futures position, they are required to deposit an *initial margin* with their brokerage or clearing firm. This initial margin represents a percentage of the total value of the futures contract. It serves as collateral to cover potential losses that may occur during the life of the contract.

2. Maintenance Margin: In addition to the initial margin, traders must also maintain a *maintenance margin*. The maintenance margin is a lower threshold set by the exchange and is typically a percentage of the initial margin. If a trader's account balance falls below the maintenance margin due to trading losses, they are required to deposit additional funds to bring it back up to the initial margin level. Failure to meet the maintenance margin requirement can lead to a margin call and potentially the forced liquidation of the trader's position.

3. Variation Margin: The *variation margin* represents the daily gains and losses on a futures position. At the end of each trading day, the clearinghouse calculates the change in the contract's value (mark-to-market) and settles these gains or losses in cash. If a trader incurs a loss, the variation margin is deducted from their account, and if they make a profit, it is added to their account.

Role of Clearinghouses

Clearinghouses, also known as *central clearing counterparties (CCPs)*, are pivotal institutions in futures markets. They serve several essential functions:

1. Counterparty Risk Mitigation: Clearinghouses act as intermediaries between buyers and sellers of futures contracts. When a trade is executed, the clearinghouse becomes the counterparty to both sides of the transaction. This arrangement eliminates counterparty risk, as traders no longer need to worry about the financial stability of their counterparts. If one party defaults on their obligations, the clearinghouse steps in to fulfill them.

2. Margin Management: Clearinghouses manage margin requirements, including initial margin and maintenance margin. They calculate and enforce these requirements for all market participants. This ensures that traders have adequate funds in their accounts to cover potential losses.

3. Daily Settlement: Clearinghouses oversee the daily settlement process. At the end of each trading day, they determine the gains and losses for each trader based on the difference between the contract's settlement price and the previous day's settlement price. These gains and losses are settled in cash, ensuring that traders have sufficient funds to cover potential losses.

4. Risk Management: Clearinghouses play a critical role in risk management. They monitor market activity and assess potential risks to the financial system. If necessary, they may implement risk-reduction measures, such as increasing margin requirements or adjusting position limits, to maintain market stability.

5. Default Management: In the rare event of a trader's default, the clearinghouse steps in to manage the default. They may use the defaulted trader's margin funds to cover losses and ensure that the non-defaulting traders do not bear the burden of the default.

Chapter 3: Options: Basics and Strategies

Basics of Option Contracts: Calls and Puts

Options provide traders and investors with unique opportunities to manage risk, speculate on price movements, and optimize their financial strategies. To begin, let's delve into the fundamentals of option contracts, specifically focusing on two primary types: calls and puts.

1. Calls and Puts: The Foundation of Options

At the heart of the options market are two fundamental contract types: *call options* and *put options*. These contracts grant their holders the right, but not the obligation, to buy (in the case of calls) or sell (in the case of puts) an underlying asset at a predetermined price (the *strike price*) on or before a specified future date (the *expiration date*).

a. Call Options

A *call option* gives its holder the right to *buy* the underlying asset at the strike price. Call options are often used when traders expect the price of the underlying asset to rise. Key features of call options include:

- **Strike Price**: The price at which the holder can buy the underlying asset.
- **Expiration Date**: The date when the option contract expires, after which it becomes worthless if not exercised.
- **Premium**: The price paid by the option holder to acquire the call option. It represents the cost of purchasing the right to buy the underlying asset.

Example: Suppose an investor holds a call option with a strike price of $100 on a stock that is currently trading at $110. If the stock's price rises to $120 before the option's expiration date, the investor can exercise the call option, buying the stock for $100 (the strike price) and immediately selling it for $120 in the market, realizing a $20 profit per share.

b. Put Options

A *put option* provides its holder with the right to *sell* the underlying asset at the strike price. Put options are often used when traders anticipate that the price of the underlying asset will fall. Key features of put options include:

- **Strike Price**: The price at which the holder can sell the underlying asset.
- **Expiration Date**: The date when the option contract expires, after which it becomes worthless if not exercised.
- **Premium**: The price paid by the option holder to acquire the put option. It represents the cost of purchasing the right to sell the underlying asset.

Example: Consider an investor who holds a put option with a strike price of $50 on a stock that is currently trading at $45. If the stock's price drops to $40 before the option's expiration date, the investor can exercise the put option, selling the stock for $50 (the strike price) in the market, even though its current market price is $40, thereby realizing a $10 profit per share.

Options Terminology

To navigate the world of options effectively, it's essential to understand some key terminology:

- **In-the-Money (ITM)**: An option is considered in-the-money if it has intrinsic value. For call options, this means the underlying asset's price is higher than the strike price. For put options, it means the underlying asset's price is lower than the strike price.
- **Out-of-the-Money (OTM)**: An option is considered out-of-the-money if it has no intrinsic value. For call options, this occurs when the underlying asset's price is lower than the strike price. For put options, it happens when the underlying asset's price is higher than the strike price.
- **At-the-Money (ATM)**: An option is at-the-money when the

underlying asset's price is approximately equal to the strike price.

Understanding these fundamental concepts is crucial for grasping the mechanics of options trading and building effective strategies. In the subsequent sections of this chapter, we will delve deeper into option strategies, including hedging, speculation, and income generation, providing you with a comprehensive understanding of how options can be used to achieve a variety of financial objectives. Join us as we continue our journey into the intricate world of options trading and investing.

Option Payoff Profiles

As we dive deeper into the world of options, one essential concept to grasp is the *option payoff profile*. Understanding how an option's value changes in response to different underlying asset prices at expiration is fundamental for traders and investors. In this section, we'll explore the payoff profiles of both call and put options, providing insights into the potential outcomes and strategies associated with each.

1. Call Option Payoff Profile

A call option's payoff profile depicts the profit or loss that the option holder can realize at the option's expiration, based on the price of the underlying asset. Here's a breakdown of the key components of a call option's payoff profile:

- **Strike Price (K)**: The price at which the option holder has the right to buy the underlying asset.
- **Premium Paid (C)**: The price paid by the option holder to acquire the call option.
- **Expiration Price of the Underlying Asset (S)**: The price of the underlying asset at the option's expiration.

The formula for calculating the profit or loss from holding a call option at expiration is:

Profit (or Loss) = Max(S - K, 0) - C

Now, let's break down the potential scenarios:

- **Scenario 1: S > K + C (In-the-Money Call Option)**

In this scenario, the price of the underlying asset at expiration is higher than the sum of the strike price and the premium paid for the call option. The option holder would likely choose to exercise the call option, buying the underlying asset at the strike price (K) and immediately selling it at the higher market price (S). The profit is equal to S - K - C, which is positive.

- **Scenario 2: S ≤ K (Out-of-the-Money Call Option)**

If the price of the underlying asset is at or below the strike price at expiration, the call option expires worthless. The option holder does not exercise the option, resulting in a loss equal to the premium paid (C).

- **Scenario 3: K < S ≤ K + C (At-the-Money Call Option)**

When the price of the underlying asset is between the strike price and the sum of the strike price and premium at expiration, the option holder may choose to exercise the option or allow it to expire. The profit or loss depends on the specific market conditions and trading costs.

2. Put Option Payoff Profile

Now, let's explore the payoff profile of a put option. A put option's payoff profile represents the potential profit or loss for the option holder at expiration, based on the price of the underlying asset. Key components of a put option's payoff profile include:

- **Strike Price (K)**: The price at which the option holder has the right to sell the underlying asset.
- **Premium Paid (P)**: The price paid by the option holder to acquire

the put option.

- **Expiration Price of the Underlying Asset (S)**: The price of the underlying asset at the option's expiration.

The formula for calculating the profit or loss from holding a put option at expiration is:

Profit (or Loss) = Max(K - S, 0) - P

Now, let's examine the potential scenarios:

- **Scenario 1: S < K - P (In-the-Money Put Option)**

In this scenario, the price of the underlying asset at expiration is lower than the difference between the strike price and the premium paid for the put option. The option holder would likely choose to exercise the put option, selling the underlying asset at the strike price (K) and immediately buying it back at the lower market price (S). The profit is equal to K - S - P, which is positive.

- **Scenario 2: S ≥ K (Out-of-the-Money Put Option)**

If the price of the underlying asset is at or above the strike price at expiration, the put option expires worthless. The option holder does not exercise the option, resulting in a loss equal to the premium paid (P).

- **Scenario 3: K - P < S ≤ K (At-the-Money Put Option)**

When the price of the underlying asset is between the strike price and the sum of the strike price and premium at expiration, the option holder may choose to exercise the option or allow it to expire. The profit or loss depends on specific market conditions and trading costs.

Understanding these payoff profiles is essential for option traders and investors to make informed decisions. These profiles serve as a foundation for constructing various option strategies, including hedging, speculating on price movements, and generating income.

Option Pricing Models: Black-Scholes and Binomial

In the world of options, pricing is a crucial component that enables traders and investors to make informed decisions. Two widely used models for pricing options are the Black-Scholes model and the Binomial model. In this section, we will delve into the principles behind these models and how they are applied to estimate option prices.

1. Black-Scholes Model

The Black-Scholes model, developed by economists Fischer Black, Myron Scholes, and Robert Merton in the early 1970s, revolutionized the field of options pricing. This model provides a mathematical framework for estimating the fair market value of European-style options, which can only be exercised at expiration. Here are the key components of the Black-Scholes model:

- **S**: The current price of the underlying asset.
- **K**: The strike price of the option.
- **T**: The time to expiration of the option, expressed in years.
- **r**: The risk-free interest rate, typically based on government bond yields.
- **σ (sigma)**: The volatility of the underlying asset's returns, representing the degree of price fluctuation.

The Black-Scholes formula for pricing a European-style call option is as follows:

*C = SN(d1) - Ke^(-rT)N(d2)

Where:

- **C** represents the call option's price.
- **N(d1)** and **N(d2)** are cumulative distribution functions of the

standard normal distribution.

- **d1** and **d2** are calculated as follows:

- $d1 = (\ln(S/K) + (r + (\sigma^2)/2)T) / (\sigma * \sqrt{T})$
- $d2 = d1 - \sigma * \sqrt{T}$

The Black-Scholes formula for pricing a European-style put option is:

$P = K * e^{(-rT)} N(-d2) - S N(-d1)$

The Black-Scholes model assumes several key assumptions:

- Efficient Markets: It assumes that markets are efficient and that there are no transaction costs.
- Constant Volatility: It assumes that the volatility of the underlying asset's returns remains constant over the option's life.
- Log-Normal Distribution: It assumes that the returns of the underlying asset follow a log-normal distribution.
- Risk-Free Interest Rate: It assumes that a risk-free interest rate exists, and it remains constant over the option's life.

2. Binomial Model

The Binomial model, also known as the Cox-Ross-Rubinstein (CRR) model, offers an alternative approach to pricing options. Unlike the Black-Scholes model, the Binomial model can be applied to a broader range of options, including American-style options that can be exercised at any time before expiration. This model is based on the concept of constructing a binomial tree of possible future prices for the underlying asset.

Here are the primary components of the Binomial model:

- **S**: The current price of the underlying asset.
- **K**: The strike price of the option.
- **T**: The time to expiration of the option, expressed in discrete periods.
- **r**: The risk-free interest rate per period.
- **u** and **d**: Multiplicative factors representing the potential up and

down movements in the underlying asset's price over each period.
- **n**: The number of periods until expiration.

The Binomial model involves constructing a binomial tree of possible asset prices at each period, calculating the option's payoff at expiration for each possible price, and then working backward through the tree to estimate the option's price at the current time.

The formula for pricing a European-style call option using the Binomial model is:

C = (Σ[Payoff at Expiration] * Probability of That Path) / (1 + r)^T

Similarly, the formula for pricing a European-style put option is:

P = (Σ[Payoff at Expiration] * Probability of That Path) / (1 + r)^T

The Binomial model's flexibility allows for the pricing of a wide range of options, including those with complex features and early exercise provisions.

Conclusion

Option pricing models like the Black-Scholes and Binomial models provide essential tools for estimating the fair market value of options. Traders and investors can use these models to make informed decisions about buying, selling, or hedging options positions. Understanding the principles and assumptions behind these models is vital for effectively navigating the world of options trading and investing.

Strategies for Hedging with Options

Hedging is a risk management technique used by investors and businesses to protect against adverse price movements in underlying assets. Options provide versatile tools for hedging strategies that help mitigate risk and ensure financial stability. In this section, we will explore several common strategies for hedging with options.

1. Protective Put Strategy

The *protective put strategy*, also known as a *married put*, involves buying a put option on an underlying asset that an investor already holds. This strategy provides downside protection by allowing the investor to sell the asset at the strike price, regardless of how low the market price may fall.

Example: Suppose an investor holds 100 shares of a tech company's stock, currently trading at $80 per share. Concerned about a potential downturn in the market, they purchase a put option with a strike price of $75 for a premium of $3 per share. If the stock price falls to $70, they can sell the stock at the strike price of $75 using the put option, limiting their losses.

2. Covered Call Strategy

The *covered call strategy* involves holding a long position in an underlying asset while simultaneously writing (selling) a call option on the same asset. This strategy generates income through the premium received from selling the call option but caps potential gains if the asset's price rises significantly.

Example: An investor owns 1,000 shares of a pharmaceutical company's stock, currently trading at $50 per share. They write (sell) call options with a strike price of $55 for a premium of $2 per share. If the stock price remains below $55, they keep the premium as income. If the stock price rises above $55, they may be obligated to sell their shares at the strike price.

3. Collar Strategy

The *collar strategy* involves simultaneously holding a long position in an underlying asset, buying a protective put option, and financing the put option by selling a covered call option. This strategy sets a price range within which the asset's price can fluctuate without incurring significant losses.

Example: An investor holds 500 shares of a utility company's stock, currently trading at $60 per share. They purchase a put option with a strike price of $55 for protection and sell a call option with a strike price of $65 to generate income. This establishes a collar with a floor at $55 and a ceiling at $65, limiting potential losses while generating premium income.

4. Long Straddle Strategy

The *long straddle strategy* involves simultaneously buying a call option and a put option with the same strike price and expiration date. This strategy is used when an investor anticipates significant price volatility in the underlying asset but is unsure about the direction of the price movement.

Example: An investor believes that a pharmaceutical company's stock, currently trading at $100, will experience a significant price swing due to an upcoming drug announcement. They buy both a call option and a put option with a strike price of $100. If the stock price moves significantly in either direction, one of the options will become profitable, potentially offsetting losses on the other option.

5. Protective Collar Strategy

The *protective collar strategy* combines elements of the protective put and covered call strategies. It involves holding a long position in an underlying asset, buying a put option for protection, and financing the put option by selling a covered call option. This strategy provides downside protection while generating income.

Example: An investor holds 1,000 shares of a technology company's stock, currently trading at $75 per share. They purchase a put option with a strike price of $70 for protection and simultaneously sell a call option with a strike price of $80 to generate income. This strategy establishes a price range between $70 and $80, protecting against losses while earning premium income.

These hedging strategies offer different ways to manage risk in various market conditions. Choosing the most suitable strategy depends on an investor's risk tolerance, market outlook, and specific objectives. By incorporating options into their portfolio, investors can enhance risk management and achieve greater financial stability.

Advanced Options Strategies: Straddles, Strangles, Spreads

In addition to basic hedging strategies, options offer a wide array of advanced strategies that traders and investors can employ to achieve specific objectives, including speculation, income generation, and risk management. In this section, we'll explore three advanced options strategies: straddles, strangles, and spreads.

1. Straddle Strategy

The *straddle strategy* is an advanced options strategy that involves simultaneously buying a call option and a put option with the same strike price and expiration date. This strategy is used when traders expect significant price volatility in the underlying asset but are uncertain about the direction of the price movement.

Key Components:

- Purchase a call option with a strike price (K).
- Purchase a put option with the same strike price (K).
- Both options have the same expiration date (T).

Objective:

- Profit from substantial price movement, regardless of whether it's up or down.

Outcome:

- If the underlying asset's price moves significantly in either direction, one of the options becomes profitable, potentially offsetting losses on the other option.
- Losses are limited to the total premium paid for both options if the asset's price remains relatively stable.

Example: Suppose a technology company is about to announce earnings, and an investor expects a significant price swing. They purchase both a call option and a put option with a strike price of $100 and an expiration date of one month. If the stock price moves significantly, one of the options will gain value, while the other may expire worthless.

2. Strangle Strategy

The *strangle strategy* is similar to the straddle but involves buying an out-of-the-money call option and an out-of-the-money put option with different strike prices. This strategy is employed when traders anticipate substantial price volatility but are uncertain about the direction of the price movement.

Key Components:

- Purchase an out-of-the-money call option with a higher strike price (K1).
- Purchase an out-of-the-money put option with a lower strike price (K2).
- Both options have the same expiration date (T).

Objective:

- Profit from significant price movement, regardless of whether it's up or down.

Outcome:

- If the underlying asset's price moves significantly in either direction, one of the options becomes profitable, potentially offsetting losses on the other option.
- Losses are limited to the total premium paid for both options if the asset's price remains relatively stable.

Example: An investor expects significant volatility in the oil market due to geopolitical events. They purchase an out-of-the-money call option with a strike price of $70 and an out-of-the-money put option with a strike price of $60, both with a one-month expiration. If the oil price experiences a substantial move, one of the options will gain value.

3. Spread Strategies

Spread strategies involve simultaneously buying and selling options on the same underlying asset but with different strike prices and/or expiration dates. These strategies are used to optimize risk-reward profiles and generate income. Two common spread strategies are the bull spread and the bear spread.

a. Bull Spread:

- **Components**: Buy a call option with a lower strike price (K1) and simultaneously sell a call option with a higher strike price (K2). Both options have the same expiration date (T).
- **Objective**: Profit from an expected moderate price increase in the underlying asset.
- **Outcome**: Gains are limited, but so are losses, making this a risk-controlled strategy.

b. Bear Spread:

- **Components**: Buy a put option with a higher strike price (K1) and simultaneously sell a put option with a lower strike price (K2). Both options have the same expiration date (T).
- **Objective**: Profit from an expected moderate price decrease in the underlying asset.
- **Outcome**: Gains are limited, but so are losses, making this a risk-controlled strategy.

Spread strategies are particularly popular for income generation and risk mitigation, as they involve both buying and selling options.

These advanced options strategies offer traders and investors greater flexibility and precision in their market approach. By understanding these strategies and their applications, individuals can tailor their options positions to match specific market conditions and objectives, ultimately enhancing their ability to navigate the complex world of options trading and investing.

Chapter 4: Trading and Valuation of Derivatives

Trading Strategies and Market Orders

In the world of derivatives, successful trading requires a deep understanding of the market, various trading strategies, and the execution of orders. In this chapter, we will explore different trading strategies commonly used in derivatives markets and how market orders play a pivotal role in executing these strategies.

1. Trading Strategies

a. Directional Strategies

1. **Long Position**: This straightforward strategy involves buying a derivative with the expectation that the underlying asset's price will rise. For example, an investor may go long on a futures contract if they anticipate a price increase in the underlying asset.
2. **Short Position**: In contrast, a short position involves selling a derivative with the expectation that the underlying asset's price will fall. Short selling is commonly used in options and futures markets to profit from declining prices.

b. Hedging Strategies

1. **Delta Hedging**: Delta hedging involves taking offsetting positions in the underlying asset and its related options to neutralize price movements. It's commonly used by options traders to manage risk.
2. **Portfolio Hedging**: Investors use derivatives to hedge their entire portfolios against adverse market movements. For example, a fund manager may use index futures to protect a diversified stock portfolio from market downturns.

c. Volatility Strategies

1. **Straddle**: As discussed in the previous chapter, a straddle involves buying both a call and a put option with the same strike price and expiration date. This strategy is used when an investor anticipates significant price volatility but is unsure about the direction of the movement.
2. **Iron Condor**: An iron condor is a strategy that combines a short straddle and a long strangle. Traders use it when they expect the underlying asset's price to remain within a specific range with low volatility.

2. Market Orders

Market orders are essential tools in derivatives trading. A market order is an instruction to execute a trade immediately at the current market price. They are known for their speed and certainty of execution. Here are some key points to understand about market orders:

- **Execution Speed**: Market orders are executed as soon as they are received by the market, making them the fastest type of order. This ensures that traders can enter or exit positions quickly.
- **Certainty of Execution**: Market orders are almost guaranteed to be executed, but the final execution price may differ slightly from the last quoted price due to market fluctuations.
- **Lack of Price Control**: Traders using market orders have limited control over the execution price. They are subject to the prevailing market bid-ask spread, which can result in price slippage.
- **Use Cases**: Market orders are commonly used when immediate execution is a higher priority than price precision. For example, during rapid market movements or for highly liquid assets, traders often prefer market orders.
- **Risk**: Market orders carry some risk of unfavorable execution prices, especially in volatile markets or with thinly traded assets. Traders should be aware of this risk and consider using limit orders in such situations.

In derivatives markets, understanding the appropriate use of market orders within various trading strategies is crucial for achieving trading objectives and managing risk effectively. Traders and investors should carefully assess the market conditions and their specific goals when deciding between market orders and other order types, such as limit orders or stop orders.

Settlement and Delivery of Derivatives

The settlement and delivery process is a critical aspect of derivatives trading, ensuring that contracts are fulfilled and obligations are met. In this chapter, we will explore how derivatives contracts are settled and delivered, including the methods and mechanisms used in different markets.

1. Settlement of Derivatives Contracts

Derivatives contracts can be settled in one of two primary ways: cash settlement or physical delivery. The choice of settlement method depends on the type of derivative and market conventions.

a. Cash Settlement

In cash settlement, the parties involved in a derivatives contract exchange cash payments based on the contract's terms, rather than physically delivering the underlying asset. Cash settlement is commonly used for contracts where the underlying asset is not easily deliverable or is not intended to change hands.

Example: Many stock index futures contracts are cash-settled. If you hold a cash-settled S&P 500 futures contract and it expires, you will receive or pay cash based on the difference between the contract's settlement price and the price at which you entered the contract.

b. Physical Delivery

Physical delivery involves the actual transfer of the underlying asset from the seller to the buyer upon contract expiration. This method is used when the underlying asset is easily deliverable, such as in the case of agricultural commodities or certain options contracts.

Example: For commodity futures contracts, like those for crude oil or wheat, physical delivery may involve the transfer of the actual commodity from the seller's storage facility to the buyer's designated location.

2. Delivery of Derivatives

a. Futures Contracts

In futures markets, both cash-settled and physically delivered contracts are common. The specifics of delivery depend on the exchange and the contract's terms. Traders and investors need to be aware of the delivery process and the requirements involved, such as the quality and quantity of the underlying asset.

b. Options Contracts

For options contracts, there are two possible scenarios regarding delivery:

- **Exercise and Assignment**: Options contract holders have the choice to exercise their options or let them expire. If an option is exercised, the writer (seller) of the option is assigned the obligation to fulfill the contract by either delivering the underlying asset (in the case of a put option) or receiving the asset (in the case of a call option).
- **Cash Settlement**: Many options contracts are cash-settled, meaning that the difference between the contract's strike price and the market price of the underlying asset at expiration is settled in cash. In this case, there is no physical delivery of the underlying asset.

c. Swaps and Other OTC Derivatives

In over-the-counter (OTC) derivatives markets, such as interest rate swaps or credit default swaps, the settlement and delivery process is determined by the terms negotiated between the parties involved. OTC derivatives are highly customizable, and settlement methods can vary widely.

3. Market Practices and Regulations

The settlement and delivery processes for derivatives are governed by market practices, exchange rules, and regulatory bodies. It is essential for participants in derivatives markets to understand and comply with these rules to ensure smooth and efficient settlement.

Conclusion

Settlement and delivery mechanisms are integral components of derivatives markets, ensuring that contracts are fulfilled in accordance with their terms. Whether through cash settlement or physical delivery, these processes provide the structure and integrity necessary for derivatives to serve as effective tools for risk management and investment. Traders and investors in derivatives should have a thorough understanding of the settlement and delivery methods relevant to their contracts and markets.

Volatility and Its Impact on Derivative Prices

Volatility plays a central role in the pricing and trading of derivatives. It refers to the degree of variation or fluctuation in the price of an underlying asset over time.

1. Understanding Volatility

Volatility can be categorized into two main types:

- **Historical Volatility**: This is calculated by analyzing past price movements of the underlying asset. It provides insight into how volatile an asset has been in the past.
- **Implied Volatility**: Implied volatility reflects the market's expectations of future price fluctuations. It is derived from the prices of options on the underlying asset and is a key input in option pricing models like the Black-Scholes model.

2. Impact of Volatility on Derivative Prices

Volatility has a significant impact on the prices of derivatives, including options and futures. Here's how it affects them:

a. Options Pricing

- **Higher Volatility Increases Option Prices**: All else being equal, higher implied volatility leads to higher option premiums. This is because higher volatility increases the probability of the underlying asset reaching a more extreme price, which can result in larger potential gains for option holders.
- **Options as Hedging Tools**: Options are often used as hedging tools to protect against adverse price movements. Traders may buy options when they expect increased volatility to shield their positions from losses.
- **Straddle and Strangle Strategies**: These strategies involve buying both call and put options (straddle) or out-of-the-money call and put options (strangle) to profit from expected volatility. Rising volatility can lead to higher profits in these strategies.

b. Futures Pricing

- **Volatility and Margin Requirements**: In futures markets, higher volatility can lead to increased margin requirements. Margin requirements are designed to cover potential losses due to price swings. As volatility rises, the potential for larger losses also increases, necessitating higher margins.
- **Speculation in Volatile Markets**: Traders who anticipate increased price volatility may enter futures contracts to speculate on price movements. For example, they may go long (buy) futures contracts when they expect prices to rise, or go short (sell) when they anticipate price declines.
- **Options on Futures**: Options on futures are also affected by volatility. Higher implied volatility leads to higher option premiums, making options more expensive for both buyers and sellers.

3. Trading Strategies in Volatile Markets

In volatile markets, traders often use specific strategies to capitalize on price fluctuations or protect against losses. Some common strategies include:

- **Straddle**: As mentioned earlier, a straddle involves buying both a call and a put option with the same strike price and expiration date. Traders use this strategy to profit from significant price swings, regardless of the direction.
- **Iron Condor**: An iron condor strategy combines a short straddle and a long strangle. Traders use it when they expect price volatility but believe that prices will stay within a specific range.
- **Volatility Index Trading**: Some traders speculate on volatility itself by trading instruments like the VIX (CBOE Volatility Index) or VIX futures and options.

Greeks: Delta, Gamma, Theta, Vega, and Rho

In the world of derivatives, understanding the Greeks is essential for traders and investors. The Greeks are a set of risk measures that quantify the sensitivity of option prices to changes in various factors, including the underlying asset's price, time to expiration, volatility, and interest rates.

1. Delta (Δ)

Delta measures the rate of change in the option price concerning changes in the underlying asset's price. It provides insight into how much an option's price is likely to change for a $1 change in the underlying asset's price. Key points about delta include:

- **Delta Range**: Delta values range from 0 to 1 for call options and -1 to 0 for put options.
- **Delta for Call Options**: A call option with a delta of 0.50 indicates that its price is expected to increase by $0.50 for every $1 increase in the underlying asset's price.
- **Delta for Put Options**: A put option with a delta of -0.50 suggests that its price is likely to decrease by $0.50 for every $1 increase in the underlying asset's price.

Delta can also be used as a measure of the option's probability of expiring in-the-money. For example, a call option with a delta of 0.70 is estimated to have a 70% chance of expiring in-the-money.

2. Gamma (Γ)

Gamma measures the rate of change in an option's delta concerning changes in the underlying asset's price. It quantifies how delta itself changes as the underlying asset's price moves. Key points about gamma include:

- **High Gamma**: Options with high gamma values exhibit sharp changes in delta when the underlying asset's price moves. These options are sensitive to price fluctuations.
- **Low Gamma**: Options with low gamma values have relatively stable delta values, indicating less sensitivity to price movements.

Traders often use gamma to assess the risk of delta hedging strategies. As the underlying asset's price changes, delta-hedged positions may need adjustment to maintain the desired risk profile.

3. Theta (Θ)

Theta measures the rate of change in an option's price concerning the passage of time. It quantifies the time decay of options, indicating how much an option's value is expected to decrease as time passes. Key points about theta include:

- **Time Decay**: Theta is a measure of time decay, meaning that options lose value as they approach expiration, all else being equal.
- **Higher Theta for Short-Term Options**: Short-term options typically have higher theta values than longer-term options, as they are more affected by time decay.

Theta is particularly important for option sellers who aim to profit from time decay. Buyers, on the other hand, must consider theta as it erodes the value of their options over time.

4. Vega (ν)

Vega measures the rate of change in an option's price concerning changes in implied volatility. It quantifies how much an option's value is expected to change for a 1% change in implied volatility. Key points about vega include:

- **Higher Vega for Longer-Term Options**: Longer-term options tend to have higher vega values than short-term options because they are more affected by changes in implied volatility.
- **Impact of Volatility**: When implied volatility rises, options with positive vega generally increase in value, and options with negative vega tend to decrease in value.

Traders often use vega to assess the impact of changes in market volatility on their options positions. It is especially relevant when trading options in response to anticipated changes in volatility.

5. Rho (ρ)

Rho measures the rate of change in an option's price concerning changes in the risk-free interest rate. It quantifies how much an option's value is expected to change for a 1% change in the interest rate. Key points about rho include:

- **Interest Rate Sensitivity**: Options with positive rho values tend to increase in value when interest rates rise, and options with negative rho values tend to decrease in value when rates rise.
- **Primarily Affects Long-Term Options**: Rho has a more significant impact on long-term options because changes in interest rates affect the present value of future cash flows.

Traders and investors use rho to gauge the sensitivity of options to changes in interest rates. It is most relevant when considering the impact of changes in rates on the pricing of options with longer maturities.

Risk-Neutral Valuation and the Role of Dividends

Risk-neutral valuation is a fundamental concept in the pricing of derivatives, especially options, and it plays a crucial role in understanding how dividends impact derivative prices.

1. Risk-Neutral Valuation

Risk-neutral valuation is a pricing approach that assumes investors are risk-neutral when it comes to holding and trading derivatives. In other words, it assumes that investors do not require any additional return for taking on the risk associated with derivatives. The risk-neutral pricing framework is particularly useful for valuing options.

Key Elements of Risk-Neutral Valuation:

- **No Risk Premium**: Risk-neutral valuation assumes that investors do not require an additional premium for taking on the risk of holding derivatives.
- **Expected Return Equals Risk-Free Rate**: In the risk-neutral world, the expected return on all assets, including derivatives, equals the risk-free interest rate.
- **Risk-Neutral Probability**: Risk-neutral valuation uses a probability distribution based on risk-neutral probabilities, where the probabilities of up and down price movements are adjusted to reflect risk-free interest rates.

2. Impact of Dividends on Derivative Pricing

Dividends play a significant role in the pricing of derivatives, especially for options on stocks. The presence of dividends affects both call and put options in different ways:

a. Call Options

- **Higher Dividends Reduce Call Option Prices**: When a stock pays dividends, the value of the dividends is expected to be received by the stockholders. Therefore, the present value of future dividends reduces the expected increase in the stock price. This, in turn, lowers the value of call options on that stock.

- **Ex-Dividend Date**: Call options are generally adjusted for dividends around the ex-dividend date, which is the date on which the stock starts trading without the right to receive the upcoming dividend. The adjustment typically involves reducing the option's price by the expected dividend amount.

b. Put Options

- **Higher Dividends Increase Put Option Prices**: For put options, dividends can have the opposite effect. Since the holder of a put option has the right to sell the stock at the strike price, higher dividends can increase the value of a put option. This is because the dividend payment effectively reduces the value of the stock, making it more likely that the stock's price will fall below the strike price.
- **American vs. European Options**: The impact of dividends on put options depends on whether the option is American or European style. American options can be exercised at any time before expiration, while European options can only be exercised at expiration. Therefore, American put options are more affected by dividends, as the option holder may choose to exercise the option to capture the dividend.

3. Dividend Yield and the Pricing Equation

The dividend yield, which is the annual dividend payment divided by the stock price, is a key factor in the pricing of options on dividend-paying stocks. The higher the dividend yield, the more significant the impact on option prices.

The pricing equation for European call options on dividend-paying stocks takes into account the dividend yield:

C = S - Xe^(-rT) - PV(D)

Where:

- **C**: Call option price
- **S**: Current stock price
- **X**: Strike price
- **e^(-rT)**: Present value factor based on the risk-free rate (T is time to expiration)
- **PV(D)**: Present value of expected dividends over the option's life

Chapter 5: Hedging with Derivatives

Risk Management and Hedging Concepts

Hedging with derivatives is a vital practice for managing risk and protecting against adverse price movements in financial markets.

1. Risk Management and Its Importance

Risk management is the process of identifying, assessing, and mitigating risks that can affect an organization's financial well-being. In financial markets, risk can take various forms, including market risk, credit risk, liquidity risk, and operational risk. Derivatives play a crucial role in managing these risks, particularly market risk.

Key Aspects of Risk Management:

- **Identification of Risks**: The first step in risk management is identifying the types of risks an organization faces, such as exposure to fluctuations in interest rates, currency exchange rates, or commodity prices.
- **Risk Assessment**: Once risks are identified, they need to be quantified and assessed in terms of potential impact and probability of occurrence.
- **Risk Mitigation**: After assessing risks, organizations can implement strategies to mitigate them. This often involves the use of derivatives to hedge against adverse price movements.
- **Monitoring and Adjustment**: Risk management is an ongoing process. Organizations must continually monitor their risk exposure and adjust their hedging strategies as market conditions change.

2. Hedging and Its Objectives

Hedging is a risk management strategy that involves using financial instruments, such as derivatives, to offset the potential losses or gains from changes in the value of underlying assets or liabilities. The primary objectives of hedging are as follows:

- **Risk Reduction**: The primary goal of hedging is to reduce or eliminate the impact of adverse price movements on a portfolio or specific assets.
- **Predictable Cash Flows**: Hedging can help create more predictable cash flows, which is essential for budgeting and financial planning.
- **Stabilizing Profits**: For businesses, hedging can stabilize profits by protecting against unfavorable market conditions.

3. Types of Risks and Corresponding Derivatives

Different types of risks require specific derivatives for effective hedging. Here are some common types of risks and the corresponding derivatives used for hedging:

- **Interest Rate Risk**: To hedge against fluctuations in interest rates, organizations use interest rate swaps, futures contracts, and options on interest rates.
- **Currency Exchange Rate Risk**: Currency forwards, options, and futures are used to hedge against exchange rate risk when dealing with international transactions.
- **Commodity Price Risk**: Commodity futures, options, and swaps are employed to hedge exposure to price movements in commodities like oil, gold, or agricultural products.
- **Equity Price Risk**: Equity options and futures can be used to hedge against stock price movements for investors and businesses with equity holdings.

4. Considerations in Hedging

Effective hedging requires careful consideration of various factors:

- **Cost of Hedging**: Hedging strategies involve costs, including transaction costs, spreads, and premiums for options. Organizations must assess whether the cost of hedging is justified by the potential risk reduction.

- **Time Horizon**: The time horizon of the hedging strategy is essential. Short-term and long-term strategies may require different derivatives and risk assessments.
- **Correlation and Diversification**: Understanding the correlation between the derivative and the underlying asset is crucial. Diversifying hedging strategies can help manage risk more effectively.
- **Regulatory and Accounting Standards**: Organizations need to adhere to regulatory and accounting standards when implementing hedging strategies. These standards may influence the choice of derivatives and reporting requirements.

Hedging with Futures Contracts

Futures contracts are powerful tools for hedging against price fluctuations in various underlying assets, including commodities, currencies, interest rates, and stock market indices.

1. Understanding Futures Contracts

A futures contract is a standardized financial derivative agreement that obligates the parties involved to buy or sell a specified quantity of an underlying asset at a predetermined price on a future date. Futures contracts are traded on organized exchanges and serve several purposes, including hedging and speculation.

Key Elements of Futures Contracts:

- **Underlying Asset**: Futures contracts are based on underlying assets, which can include commodities (e.g., crude oil, gold), financial instruments (e.g., stock indices, interest rates), or even weather conditions.
- **Contract Specifications**: Each futures contract has specific terms and conditions, including the contract size, expiration date, and

delivery location.

- **Long and Short Positions**: Futures traders can take either a long (buy) or short (sell) position in a contract. Long positions profit from rising prices, while short positions profit from falling prices.

2. Hedging with Futures Contracts

Hedging with futures contracts involves taking an offsetting position in the futures market to mitigate the risk of adverse price movements in the underlying asset. This strategy is commonly employed by businesses and investors to protect against price volatility.

Examples of Hedging with Futures:

- **Commodity Producers**: Companies that produce commodities like wheat or oil can hedge against falling prices by selling futures contracts. If prices decline, the gains in the futures market offset the losses in the physical market.
- **Importers and Exporters**: Importers and exporters can use currency futures to hedge against exchange rate fluctuations. For instance, a U.S. company importing goods from Europe can hedge against a strengthening euro by buying euro futures contracts.
- **Portfolio Managers**: Portfolio managers may use stock index futures to hedge their equity portfolios. If they anticipate a market downturn, they can take short positions in stock index futures to offset potential losses in their stock holdings.

3. Mechanics of Hedging with Futures

To effectively hedge with futures contracts, one must consider the following steps:

- **Identify the Risk**: Determine the specific risk exposure that needs to be hedged. This could be related to price changes in commodities, interest rates, foreign exchange rates, or other factors.

- **Select the Appropriate Futures Contract**: Choose the futures contract that closely matches the characteristics of the underlying asset and aligns with the hedging objectives.
- **Determine the Hedge Ratio**: Calculate the number of futures contracts needed to offset the risk exposure. The hedge ratio is typically based on the correlation between the futures price and the underlying asset's price.
- **Monitor and Adjust**: Continuously monitor the futures position and the underlying asset's performance. Adjust the hedge as needed to maintain the desired risk profile.

4. Advantages and Considerations

Hedging with futures contracts offers several advantages:

- **Risk Mitigation**: Futures contracts provide an effective means of reducing or eliminating exposure to price fluctuations, thus protecting against potential losses.
- **Price Transparency**: Futures markets offer price transparency, allowing hedgers to access real-time market prices.

However, it's important to consider factors such as transaction costs, margin requirements, and the potential for imperfect correlation between futures and the underlying asset.

Hedging with Options Contracts

Options contracts provide versatile tools for hedging against price fluctuations, and they offer unique advantages compared to futures contracts.

1. Understanding Options Contracts

Options contracts grant the holder the right, but not the obligation, to buy (call option) or sell (put option) a specific underlying asset at a predetermined price (strike price) on or before a specified expiration date. Options are traded on organized exchanges and can be used for various purposes, including hedging.

Key Elements of Options Contracts:

- **Call Options**: Call options give the holder the right to buy the underlying asset at the strike price.
- **Put Options**: Put options give the holder the right to sell the underlying asset at the strike price.
- **Expiration Date**: Options have a fixed expiration date, after which they become worthless.
- **Strike Price**: The strike price is the price at which the underlying asset can be bought or sold.
- **Premium**: The premium is the price paid to acquire the option contract.

2. Hedging with Options Contracts

Hedging with options contracts involves using options to offset potential losses or gains in the value of an underlying asset. Options offer unique advantages in hedging compared to futures contracts:

- **Limited Risk**: When purchasing options, the maximum potential loss is limited to the premium paid for the option. This makes options an attractive choice for risk-averse hedgers.
- **Flexibility**: Options provide flexibility in designing hedging strategies. Hedgers can choose from various strike prices and expiration dates to tailor the hedge to their specific needs.

Examples of Hedging with Options:

- **Stock Portfolio Protection**: Investors can purchase put options on individual stocks or stock indices to protect their portfolios against market downturns.
- **Commodity Price Risk**: Businesses involved in commodities can use options to hedge against price fluctuations. For instance, a wheat producer can purchase put options to hedge against falling wheat prices.

- **Interest Rate Risk**: Organizations can use interest rate options to hedge against changes in interest rates, protecting themselves from adverse movements in borrowing costs.

3. Mechanics of Hedging with Options

Hedging with options involves selecting the appropriate option type (call or put) and constructing a position that offsets the risk exposure in the underlying asset. Key steps in options hedging include:

- **Identify the Risk**: Determine the specific risk exposure that needs to be hedged, such as a decline in the value of a stock portfolio or an increase in interest rates.
- **Select the Appropriate Option**: Choose the type (call or put), strike price, and expiration date of the option that aligns with the hedging objectives.
- **Determine the Hedge Ratio**: Calculate the number of options contracts needed to offset the risk exposure. The hedge ratio depends on factors like the delta of the option and the correlation between the option and the underlying asset.
- **Monitor and Adjust**: Continuously monitor the performance of the options position and make adjustments as necessary to maintain the desired risk profile.

4. Advantages and Considerations

Hedging with options contracts offers several advantages:

- **Limited Risk**: Options provide downside protection with a known and limited maximum loss (the premium paid).
- **Tailored Strategies**: Options allow for precise customization of hedging strategies to address specific risk exposures.

However, it's essential to consider factors such as option premiums, time decay (theta), and implied volatility when implementing options-based hedging strategies.

Cross-Hedging and Basis Risk

Cross-hedging is a sophisticated risk management strategy that involves using derivatives to hedge against risks associated with an underlying asset that may not have a directly matching derivative contract available. In the context of cross-hedging, we'll also explore the concept of basis risk, which is an important consideration in this strategy.

1. Understanding Cross-Hedging

Cross-hedging is employed when there is no perfect or closely correlated derivative available for the specific asset or risk that needs to be hedged. Instead, a related, but not identical, derivative is used to mitigate exposure to price fluctuations.

Examples of Cross-Hedging:

- **Currency Risk for Commodities**: Consider a company that exports agricultural products and faces currency risk due to fluctuations in exchange rates. Since there may not be currency derivatives directly linked to these specific commodities, the company might use currency futures or options on currency pairs to hedge its foreign exchange risk.
- **Interest Rate Risk for Corporate Bonds**: A portfolio manager holding a collection of corporate bonds may need to hedge against rising interest rates. While there are interest rate futures and options, the bonds' interest rate risk may not perfectly match available interest rate derivatives. Cross-hedging could involve using Treasury bond futures, which are correlated but not identical to the corporate bonds, to hedge against interest rate movements.

2. Basis Risk in Cross-Hedging

Basis risk is the risk that arises when the hedge (the derivative instrument) does not perfectly correlate with the underlying asset being hedged. It results from differences in the price movements between the derivative and the asset being hedged. Basis risk can undermine the effectiveness of the hedge.

Factors Contributing to Basis Risk:

- **Divergence in Price Movements**: Even related assets may not move in perfect sync, leading to differences in price changes.
- **Maturity Mismatch**: In some cases, the maturity of the derivative may not match the maturity of the underlying asset, introducing a timing mismatch.
- **Differences in Liquidity**: The derivative and the underlying asset may have varying levels of liquidity, affecting their price movements differently.

Managing Basis Risk:

- **Diversification**: Diversifying the portfolio of derivatives used for cross-hedging can help mitigate basis risk by reducing reliance on a single derivative.
- **Regular Monitoring**: Continuously monitoring the correlation between the hedge and the underlying asset is crucial. Adjustments to the hedge can be made as needed.
- **Sophisticated Models**: Employing advanced quantitative models can aid in assessing and managing basis risk.

3. The Importance of Expertise

Cross-hedging, due to its complexity and the potential for basis risk, requires a high level of expertise in risk management and derivatives trading. Organizations often rely on financial professionals, including risk managers and derivatives specialists, to implement cross-hedging strategies effectively.

Real-world Case Studies in Effective Hedging

The application of hedging strategies in real-world scenarios can provide valuable insights into how organizations and investors use derivatives to manage risk effectively. In this section, we will explore several real-world case studies that illustrate successful hedging practices.

1. Southwest Airlines - Fuel Price Hedging

Background: Southwest Airlines, a major U.S. carrier, is known for its successful fuel price hedging strategy. Jet fuel prices are a significant cost component for airlines, and they can be highly volatile due to geopolitical events, weather disruptions, and other factors.

Hedging Strategy: Southwest Airlines implemented a proactive fuel price hedging program. They used financial derivatives, specifically futures and options contracts on crude oil, to lock in prices for a substantial portion of their future jet fuel needs. This helped the airline stabilize its fuel costs and avoid the full impact of oil price spikes.

Outcome: Southwest's hedging strategy proved effective in mitigating the impact of surging oil prices during times of geopolitical tension or supply disruptions. It provided the airline with a competitive advantage by offering more stable ticket prices compared to competitors that did not employ similar hedging practices.

2. Archer Daniels Midland (ADM) - Agricultural Commodity Hedging

Background: ADM is a global leader in agricultural processing, and its operations are heavily influenced by fluctuations in commodity prices. The company processes and trades in commodities like corn, soybeans, and wheat.

Hedging Strategy: ADM uses a combination of futures and options contracts to hedge against price volatility in the agricultural commodities market. They carefully assess their risk exposure to fluctuations in commodity prices and use derivatives to lock in favorable prices for future purchases and sales.

Outcome: ADM's hedging strategy helps them maintain stable profit margins despite the inherent price volatility in the agricultural commodities market. It provides a level of predictability in their financial performance and minimizes the impact of adverse price movements.

3. Apple Inc. - Foreign Exchange Hedging

Background: Apple Inc., a global technology giant, conducts a significant portion of its business internationally. This exposes the company to currency exchange rate risk, as fluctuations in exchange rates can impact revenues and costs.

Hedging Strategy: Apple employs currency hedging strategies to protect against adverse movements in exchange rates. They use derivatives, including currency forwards and options, to hedge currency exposure related to their international operations. This allows Apple to lock in favorable exchange rates for future transactions.

Outcome: Apple's currency hedging practices help stabilize its financial performance by reducing the impact of unfavorable exchange rate movements. This ensures that the company's revenues and costs remain relatively predictable, even in the face of currency market volatility.

Chapter 6: Speculation and Trading Strategies

Speculation vs. Investment

In the realm of financial markets, speculation and investment are two distinct approaches to allocating capital with different objectives, time horizons, and risk profiles.

1. Speculation

Definition: Speculation involves making financial decisions with the primary goal of profiting from short- to medium-term price fluctuations in assets, such as stocks, bonds, commodities, or currencies. Speculators are driven by the anticipation of price movements, and their strategies often involve higher levels of risk and leverage.

Characteristics of Speculation:

- **Short-Term Focus**: Speculators typically have a short-term investment horizon, aiming to capitalize on market inefficiencies or sentiment-driven price swings.
- **High Risk Tolerance**: Speculators are often willing to take on higher levels of risk in pursuit of potentially substantial gains.
- **Leverage**: Leveraging borrowed capital to amplify potential returns (or losses) is common among speculators, especially in derivatives markets.
- **Diverse Strategies**: Speculators employ a wide range of strategies, including day trading, swing trading, and options trading, to capitalize on market volatility.
- **Market Timing**: Successful speculation often hinges on accurately timing market entry and exit points to profit from anticipated price movements.

2. Investment

Definition: Investment involves deploying capital with the objective of generating long-term wealth accumulation or income. Investors adopt a more patient and less speculative approach, seeking to build wealth gradually through asset appreciation and/or dividend or interest income.

Characteristics of Investment:

- **Long-Term Focus**: Investors have a longer investment horizon, often spanning years or even decades. They aim to benefit from the compound growth of their investments over time.
- **Risk Management**: Investors prioritize preserving capital and mitigating risk. They typically avoid excessive leverage and focus on asset diversification.
- **Fundamental Analysis**: Investors frequently conduct in-depth fundamental analysis to evaluate the financial health and growth potential of the assets they hold.
- **Passive Strategies**: Many investors opt for passive strategies, such as buy-and-hold investing or index fund investing, to minimize trading activity and transaction costs.
- **Income Generation**: Some investors focus on income-generating assets, like dividend stocks or bonds, to receive regular cash flows.

3. Speculation vs. Investment

The key distinctions between speculation and investment lie in their objectives, time horizons, and risk attitudes:

- **Objective**: Speculators aim to profit from price fluctuations, while investors aim for long-term wealth accumulation or income generation.
- **Time Horizon**: Speculators have a short- to medium-term outlook, whereas investors adopt a long-term perspective.
- **Risk Profile**: Speculation carries higher inherent risk due to its focus on short-term price movements and leverage. Investment tends to prioritize risk management and wealth preservation.

Speculative Strategies: Long and Short Positions

In the realm of financial markets, traders and speculators employ a variety of strategies to profit from price movements in assets. Two fundamental speculative strategies are taking long positions and short positions.

1. Long Position

Definition: A long position, often referred to as "going long," involves buying an asset with the expectation that its price will rise over time. When an investor or trader takes a long position, they aim to profit from the appreciation of the asset's value.

Objectives of Long Position:

- **Capital Appreciation**: The primary objective of going long is to benefit from the asset's price increasing, leading to capital appreciation.
- **Income Generation**: Some long positions, such as dividend-paying stocks or interest-bearing bonds, also provide income through dividends or interest payments.

Mechanics of a Long Position:

1. **Purchase**: The trader or investor buys the asset at the current market price.
2. **Holding**: The asset is held in the portfolio for an extended period, often with a long-term investment horizon.
3. **Profit Realization**: The long position becomes profitable if the asset's price rises. At this point, the trader can choose to sell the asset to realize the profit.

2. Short Position

Definition: A short position, often referred to as "going short" or "shorting," involves selling an asset that the trader does not own with the expectation that its price will decline. When a trader takes a short position, they aim to profit from falling asset prices.

Objectives of Short Position:

- **Profit from Price Decline:** The primary goal of going short is to profit as the asset's price falls, enabling the trader to buy it back at a lower price.

Mechanics of a Short Position:

1. **Borrow and Sell:** The trader borrows the asset from a broker or another source and sells it in the market at the current market price.
2. **Waiting for Price Decline:** The trader holds the short position and waits for the asset's price to decline, aiming to buy it back later at a lower price.
3. **Profit Realization:** The short position becomes profitable when the asset's price falls. To realize the profit, the trader buys back the asset at the reduced price and returns it to the lender.

Risks and Considerations:

- Short positions involve unlimited potential losses if the asset's price rises significantly, as the trader must buy it back at a higher price.
- Borrowing fees and interest charges may apply when shorting assets.

Arbitrage Opportunities in Derivative Markets

Arbitrage is a trading strategy that aims to profit from price discrepancies of identical or similar assets in different markets. In derivative markets, arbitrage opportunities are prevalent due to the interconnected nature of financial instruments. In this section, we will explore the concept of arbitrage in derivative markets, its types, and how traders capitalize on these opportunities.

1. Understanding Arbitrage

Definition: Arbitrage is the practice of simultaneously buying and selling an asset (or related assets) in different markets to take advantage of price differentials. The goal is to generate a risk-free profit by exploiting temporary market inefficiencies.

Arbitrage Opportunities in Derivative Markets: Arbitrage can be particularly attractive in derivative markets, where various financial instruments are interconnected. Common types of arbitrage in derivative markets include:

- **Spatial Arbitrage**: Exploiting price differences for the same derivative contract on different exchanges. Traders buy on the exchange with the lower price and sell on the exchange with the higher price.
- **Temporal Arbitrage**: Capitalizing on price variations for the same derivative over time. For instance, a trader may buy a futures contract expiring in the distant future and sell the same asset in the spot market, expecting the futures price to converge with the spot price over time.
- **Statistical Arbitrage**: Using quantitative models to identify mispriced assets or relationships between assets and take positions that profit from price adjustments.

2. Triangular Arbitrage in Forex Markets

One of the most well-known forms of arbitrage occurs in the foreign exchange (forex) market and is known as triangular arbitrage. It involves exploiting exchange rate discrepancies between three currency pairs to make a risk-free profit. Here's a simplified example:

- Currency Pair 1: EUR/USD
- Currency Pair 2: USD/JPY
- Currency Pair 3: EUR/JPY

Suppose that the exchange rates are as follows:

- EUR/USD: 1.1000
- USD/JPY: 108.00

- EUR/JPY: 118.80

If a trader notices that EUR/JPY is trading at 118.80 on one exchange but finds that buying EUR/USD at 1.1000 and then buying USD/JPY at 108.00 would yield a lower rate than 118.80, they can arbitrage the difference. They would buy EUR/USD, then USD/JPY, effectively selling EUR/JPY at a higher rate than they bought it, thereby making a profit.

3. Risk and Execution

While arbitrage opportunities seem risk-free in theory, they are not entirely without risk in practice. Several factors can introduce risk:

- Execution Risk: Markets move quickly, and prices can change before an arbitrage opportunity is fully executed.
- Transaction Costs: Trading costs, such as commissions and spreads, can erode profits.
- Model Risk: Statistical arbitrage strategies relying on quantitative models are subject to model risk, where model assumptions may not hold.

Algorithmic and High-Frequency Trading

In today's financial markets, technology has revolutionized the way trading is conducted. Algorithmic trading and high-frequency trading (HFT) are two prominent strategies that rely on computer algorithms and rapid execution to gain a competitive edge. In this section, we will delve into these trading approaches, their mechanics, and their impact on modern markets.

1. Algorithmic Trading

Definition: Algorithmic trading, often referred to as algo trading, involves the use of computer algorithms to automate trading decisions and execute orders. These algorithms are designed to analyze market data, identify trading opportunities, and execute trades at optimal prices and speeds.

Key Characteristics:

- **Speed**: Algorithmic trading systems can execute trades at speeds measured in microseconds, allowing for rapid responses to market conditions.
- **Precision**: Algorithms are programmed to execute trades with precision, adhering to predefined criteria and risk management rules.
- **Diversification**: Algo traders can simultaneously manage and execute trades across multiple asset classes and markets.

Strategies: Algorithmic trading encompasses various strategies, including:

- **Market Making**: Providing liquidity to the market by continuously quoting buy and sell prices, profiting from the bid-ask spread.
- **Statistical Arbitrage**: Identifying mispricings between related assets and taking advantage of price disparities.
- **Trend Following**: Trading based on trends identified through technical analysis.
- **Execution Algorithms**: Algorithms designed to execute large orders efficiently without causing significant market impact.

2. High-Frequency Trading (HFT)

Definition: High-frequency trading is a subset of algorithmic trading characterized by extremely rapid order execution, often measured in nanoseconds. HFT firms use advanced technology and infrastructure to capitalize on small price discrepancies and market inefficiencies.

Key Characteristics:

- **Ultra-Fast Execution**: HFT firms invest heavily in low-latency technology and co-location to execute orders at lightning speed.
- **Low Holding Periods**: HFT strategies typically involve holding positions for very short durations, sometimes just milliseconds.
- **Market Data Analysis**: HFT algorithms analyze vast amounts of market data to identify fleeting opportunities for profit.

Strategies: High-frequency trading strategies include:

- **Market-Making**: Similar to traditional market makers but with a focus on rapid order execution and tight spreads.
- **Arbitrage**: Identifying and exploiting price discrepancies between different markets or asset classes.
- **Statistical Arbitrage**: Leveraging mathematical models to identify short-term pricing anomalies.

Impact on Markets:

HFT has had a significant impact on modern financial markets:

- **Increased Liquidity**: HFT firms often act as liquidity providers, enhancing market liquidity.
- **Reduced Spreads**: HFT can lead to narrower bid-ask spreads, benefiting retail investors.
- **Market Fragmentation**: The rise of HFT has contributed to the fragmentation of markets across multiple trading venues.

The Psychology of Speculation and Risk Management

Successful speculation and effective risk management in financial markets are not solely determined by quantitative analysis and strategies; they also heavily depend on understanding and managing the psychological aspects of trading. In this section, we will delve into the psychology of speculation, common psychological biases, and the importance of disciplined risk management.

1. The Psychology of Speculation

Emotions in Trading: Emotions often play a significant role in trading decisions. Common emotions experienced by traders include:

- **Greed**: The desire for quick profits can lead to overtrading and excessive risk-taking.
- **Fear**: Fear of losses can result in premature exits from profitable

trades or avoiding potentially lucrative opportunities.

- **Overconfidence**: Excessive self-assuredness can lead to overleveraging and ignoring risk.
- **Regret Aversion**: The fear of regret can influence traders to hold losing positions for too long, hoping they will turn profitable.

Discipline and Self-Control: Successful speculators cultivate discipline and self-control to manage their emotions. This includes sticking to trading plans, setting predefined entry and exit points, and not deviating from risk management rules.

2. Psychological Biases in Trading

Confirmation Bias: Traders often seek information that confirms their existing beliefs or biases, leading to selective perception of news and analysis.

Loss Aversion: The aversion to losses can result in traders holding losing positions longer than they should or taking excessive risks to recover losses.

Anchoring: Traders may anchor their decisions to a specific price or event, leading to irrational trading behavior when market conditions change.

Herd Mentality: The tendency to follow the crowd can result in mass market movements driven by emotions rather than rational analysis.

Overtrading: Impulsive and frequent trading, often driven by boredom or a desire for action, can lead to higher transaction costs and losses.

3. Risk Management and Position Sizing

Position Sizing: Effective risk management involves determining the appropriate size of each trade based on factors like account size, risk tolerance, and the specific trade's risk-reward profile. Proper position sizing helps protect capital and mitigate the impact of losses.

Stop Loss Orders: Traders use stop loss orders to limit potential losses by automatically exiting a position if it reaches a predefined price level. This tool is crucial for risk management.

Diversification: Spreading investments across different assets or markets can help reduce risk by minimizing the impact of poor-performing positions.

4. Mindfulness and Emotional Intelligence

Mindfulness: Mindfulness techniques, such as meditation and deep breathing exercises, can help traders stay calm, focused, and less reactive to emotional impulses.

Emotional Intelligence: Developing emotional intelligence allows traders to better understand and manage their emotions, which is vital for making rational decisions in high-pressure trading environments.

Chapter 7: Interest Rate Derivatives

Introduction to Interest Rate Swaps

Interest rate derivatives are financial instruments that derive their value from changes in interest rates. Among these derivatives, interest rate swaps are among the most widely used. In this section, we will introduce interest rate swaps, explain their mechanics, and explore their applications.

1. What is an Interest Rate Swap?

An interest rate swap is a financial contract between two parties that involves the exchange of interest payments. These payments are typically based on a notional principal amount. In an interest rate swap, the two primary types of interest payments being exchanged are:

- **Fixed Interest Payments**: One party agrees to pay a fixed interest rate.
- **Floating Interest Payments**: The other party agrees to pay a variable, or floating, interest rate, often linked to a reference rate such as the London Interbank Offered Rate (LIBOR) or the U.S. Federal Funds Rate.

2. Mechanics of an Interest Rate Swap

The basic mechanics of an interest rate swap involve the following steps:

- **Contract Agreement**: Two parties agree to enter into an interest rate swap contract, specifying the notional principal amount, the fixed interest rate, the floating interest rate, and the payment frequency.
- **Interest Payments**: At regular intervals (e.g., quarterly or annually), interest payments are calculated based on the notional principal amount, the fixed rate, and the floating rate.
- **Payment Exchange**: The party paying the fixed interest rate makes payments based on the fixed rate, while the party paying the floating

interest rate makes payments based on the current floating rate.

- **Net Settlement**: The party paying the lower interest amount receives a net payment from the other party. This net payment is the difference between the fixed and floating interest payments.

3. Purposes and Applications of Interest Rate Swaps

Interest rate swaps serve various purposes and are applied in a range of financial scenarios:

- **Hedging Interest Rate Risk**: Organizations use interest rate swaps to hedge against interest rate fluctuations. For example, a company with variable-rate debt might enter into an interest rate swap to convert its variable interest payments into fixed payments.
- **Optimizing Borrowing Costs**: Entities can use swaps to optimize their borrowing costs. For instance, a company might have a comparative advantage in borrowing at fixed rates but prefers floating-rate debt. By using an interest rate swap, it can achieve its preferred interest rate structure.
- **Managing Asset and Liability Mismatch**: Financial institutions may use interest rate swaps to align the maturities and interest rate structures of their assets and liabilities, reducing the risk of interest rate mismatches.
- **Speculation**: Some investors and traders use interest rate swaps for speculative purposes, betting on the future direction of interest rates.

4. Risks Associated with Interest Rate Swaps

While interest rate swaps can be valuable tools for managing interest rate exposure, they also carry certain risks, including:

- **Counterparty Risk**: The risk that one party may default on its payment obligations, leading to financial losses for the other party.
- **Market Risk**: Changes in interest rates can affect the market value of interest rate swaps. When rates move unfavorably, the value of the

swap may decline.

- **Basis Risk:** Basis risk arises when the floating rate used in the swap is linked to a different benchmark than the entity's actual interest rate exposure.

Forward Rate Agreements (FRAs)

Interest rate derivatives play a crucial role in the financial markets, allowing participants to manage and hedge interest rate risk effectively. Among these derivatives, Forward Rate Agreements (FRAs) stand out as versatile instruments that enable parties to secure interest rates for future periods, providing a means to mitigate risk and gain insight into future interest rate movements.

Understanding Forward Rate Agreements (FRAs)

At its core, a Forward Rate Agreement (FRA) is a financial contract between two parties that allows them to establish a predetermined interest rate for a specified future period. These agreements facilitate risk management by locking in interest rates, providing certainty in an uncertain financial landscape.

Key Elements of FRAs:

1. **Notional Amount**: The notional amount represents the principal on which interest rate payments are calculated. It's important to note that the notional amount is not exchanged between the parties; rather, it serves as the basis for calculating interest payments.
2. **Fixed Rate**: In an FRA, one party agrees to pay a fixed interest rate, which is determined at the inception of the agreement. This fixed rate remains constant throughout the contract period.
3. **Floating Rate**: The counterparty commits to paying a floating interest rate, typically tied to a benchmark interest rate such as the London Interbank Offered Rate (LIBOR) or EURIBOR. The floating rate payment is based on the reference rate's value at the start of the specified period.
4. **Contract Period**: FRAs have a predefined contract period

representing the duration over which the interest rate agreement is effective. This period is typically set to align with the frequency of interest rate resets for the floating reference rate, such as three or six months.

Mechanics of Forward Rate Agreements (FRAs)

The mechanics of an FRA involve a series of steps:

1. **Contract Formation**: Two parties, often referred to as the "buyer" and "seller" of the FRA, enter into the agreement. They agree on the notional amount, fixed interest rate, floating reference rate, and contract period.
2. **Calculation Period**: The contract period is divided into sub-periods, typically matching the frequency of interest rate resets for the floating reference rate. For example, if the floating rate is reset every three months, the contract period may be divided into quarters.
3. **Interest Calculation**: At the end of each sub-period, the fixed interest rate is applied to the notional amount. This calculation determines the interest payment owed by one party to the other.
4. **Payment Settlement**: On the settlement date, which usually occurs at the beginning of the contract period, the party obligated to pay the fixed interest amount transfers the payment to the counterparty. Simultaneously, the party obligated to pay the floating rate pays the calculated amount based on the prevailing floating reference rate.
5. **Net Settlement**: In some cases, the fixed and floating interest rates may not be equal. When this occurs, the party owing the higher interest payment will make a net payment to the other party, representing the difference between the two payments.

Purposes and Applications of FRAs

FRAs serve diverse purposes and find applications in various financial scenarios:

1. **Hedging Interest Rate Risk**: One of the primary uses of FRAs is to

hedge against interest rate fluctuations. Suppose a company has an upcoming financing requirement but wants to protect itself from rising interest rates. In that case, it can enter into an FRA to secure a fixed interest rate, ensuring predictable future borrowing costs.

2. **Speculation**: Traders and investors often use FRAs to express views on future interest rate movements. For instance, if an investor anticipates a decline in interest rates, they may enter into an FRA agreement with a fixed rate lower than the expected future floating rate, aiming to profit from the rate differential.
3. **Asset and Liability Management**: Financial institutions, including banks, use FRAs to align the interest rate profiles of their assets and liabilities. By managing their interest rate exposure with FRAs, these institutions can mitigate the risk associated with fluctuations in market interest rates.
4. **Arbitrage**: Arbitrageurs may use FRAs to exploit pricing discrepancies between the FRA market and other interest rate instruments, taking advantage of potential mispricings for profit.

Pricing and Valuation of Interest Rate Options

Interest rate options are derivative contracts that provide the holder with the right, but not the obligation, to buy or sell an underlying interest rate instrument at a predetermined strike rate on or before a specified maturity date. These options play a pivotal role in managing interest rate risk and speculating on interest rate movements. In this section, we will explore the pricing and valuation of interest rate options, shedding light on the intricate calculations and factors that determine their value.

1. Understanding Interest Rate Options

Interest rate options come in two primary forms: interest rate call options and interest rate put options.

- **Interest Rate Call Option**: This option gives the holder the right to buy an underlying interest rate instrument at a predetermined strike rate.

- **Interest Rate Put Option**: This option provides the holder with the right to sell an underlying interest rate instrument at a predetermined strike rate.

Interest rate options are typically European-style, meaning they can be exercised only at maturity. They are also cash-settled, meaning that no physical delivery of the underlying instrument occurs; instead, the difference between the strike rate and the market rate at maturity determines the cash settlement.

2. Factors Affecting Interest Rate Option Pricing

Several key factors influence the pricing and valuation of interest rate options:

- **Interest Rate Levels**: The current level of interest rates significantly impacts option pricing. Higher interest rates tend to increase the value of call options but decrease the value of put options, and vice versa.
- **Strike Rate**: The strike rate, also known as the exercise price, is the rate at which the option holder can buy (for call options) or sell (for put options) the underlying instrument. The relationship between the strike rate and the prevailing market rate affects option pricing.
- **Time to Maturity**: The longer the time to maturity, the higher the option premium, as there is a greater opportunity for market rate movements that can benefit the option holder.
- **Volatility**: Increased volatility in interest rates generally leads to higher option premiums. This reflects the uncertainty surrounding future interest rate movements.
- **Interest Rate Models**: Various mathematical models, such as the Black-Scholes model and the Binomial model, are used to calculate option prices. These models consider the factors mentioned above and incorporate them into option pricing formulas.

3. Black-Scholes Model for Interest Rate Options

The Black-Scholes model, originally developed for pricing equity options, can be adapted for interest rate options. The model provides a theoretical framework for estimating the fair value of these options. The key components of the Black-Scholes model for interest rate options include:

- **Underlying Interest Rate Instrument**: The specific interest rate instrument (e.g., Treasury bonds) upon which the option is based.
- **Strike Rate**: The predetermined rate at which the option holder can buy (for call options) or sell (for put options) the underlying instrument.
- **Time to Maturity**: The time remaining until the option's expiration date.
- **Volatility**: The historical and expected future volatility of interest rates.
- **Risk-Free Interest Rate**: The prevailing risk-free interest rate in the market, often represented by government bond yields.

Using these inputs, the Black-Scholes model calculates the option's theoretical value, known as the option premium. This premium represents the price a buyer should be willing to pay to acquire the option.

4. Valuation and Risk Management

Valuing interest rate options is essential for risk management and decision-making. Option traders and investors use option pricing models like Black-Scholes to determine the fair value of options in their portfolios.

Additionally, delta, gamma, theta, vega, and rho—known as the "Greeks"—are metrics used to assess how sensitive an option's price is to changes in underlying factors like interest rates, time to maturity, and volatility. Understanding the Greeks is crucial for managing and adjusting option positions to align with desired risk profiles.

Managing Interest Rate Risk with Derivatives

Interest rate risk is a significant concern for individuals, businesses, and financial institutions alike. Fluctuations in interest rates can impact borrowing costs, investment returns, and overall financial stability. To mitigate this risk, market participants turn to derivatives—financial instruments whose values are derived from underlying interest rates. In this section, we will delve into the ways derivatives can be used to manage interest rate risk effectively.

1. Interest Rate Risk: A Brief Overview

Interest rate risk refers to the potential for financial losses or gains due to changes in interest rates. Two primary components of interest rate risk are:

- **Price Risk**: The risk that changes in interest rates will impact the value of fixed-income investments, such as bonds.
- **Reinvestment Risk**: The risk that future cash flows from fixed-income investments cannot be reinvested at the same rate as the original investment.

Interest rate risk can affect both borrowers and lenders:

- Borrowers are concerned about the potential increase in borrowing costs if interest rates rise.
- Lenders, on the other hand, are concerned about the impact of falling interest rates on their income and the value of their fixed-income investments.

2. Using Derivatives to Manage Interest Rate Risk

Derivatives offer several strategies to manage interest rate risk:

- **Interest Rate Swaps**: As discussed earlier, interest rate swaps enable parties to exchange fixed and floating interest rate payments. For borrowers, this can help convert variable-rate debt to fixed-rate debt to shield against rising interest rates. For investors, swaps can be used to enhance yield by exchanging fixed-rate income for floating-rate income when rates are expected to fall.

- **Interest Rate Futures and Options**: These derivatives provide a means to hedge or speculate on future interest rate movements. For example, if a borrower expects rates to rise, they can buy interest rate futures or options to offset potential interest cost increases.
- **Caps and Floors**: Interest rate caps protect borrowers from rising interest rates by capping the maximum rate they would pay. Conversely, interest rate floors protect lenders by setting a minimum rate they would receive. These options can be customized to suit specific interest rate risk management needs.
- **Forward Rate Agreements (FRAs)**: FRAs allow parties to lock in future interest rates, providing certainty for borrowing or lending. For example, a borrower can enter into an FRA to fix the interest rate on a future loan, guarding against rate increases.

3. Risk Management Strategies

Managing interest rate risk effectively requires careful consideration of an organization's financial position and objectives. Here are some key strategies:

- **Asset-Liability Management (ALM)**: Financial institutions, such as banks and insurance companies, use ALM to align the maturities and interest rate structures of their assets and liabilities. This helps mitigate interest rate risk by reducing mismatches.
- **Duration Matching**: Investors can use duration—a measure of a bond's sensitivity to interest rate changes—to match the duration of their investments with their anticipated liability durations. This strategy minimizes the impact of interest rate fluctuations on investment portfolios.
- **Stress Testing**: Stress testing involves modeling the impact of extreme interest rate scenarios on a portfolio. This helps organizations assess their vulnerability to sudden rate changes and implement risk mitigation measures accordingly.

4. Monitoring and Adjusting Strategies

Interest rate risk management is an ongoing process. Market participants must continually monitor the interest rate environment and adjust their strategies as needed. This may involve periodic rebalancing of investment portfolios, evaluating the need for hedging instruments, and staying informed about economic indicators that can signal potential interest rate shifts.

The Role of Interest Rate Derivatives in Monetary Policy

Interest rate derivatives play a significant and multifaceted role in the implementation and transmission of monetary policy. Central banks, as the custodians of monetary policy, utilize these derivatives to influence and regulate key interest rates in the financial system. In this section, we will explore the essential role of interest rate derivatives in monetary policy and their impact on financial markets.

1. Monetary Policy Tools

Monetary policy is the process by which central banks manage the money supply and interest rates to achieve economic objectives such as price stability, full employment, and sustainable economic growth. Central banks employ a range of tools to implement monetary policy, including:

- **Open Market Operations**: Central banks buy or sell government securities in the open market to influence the money supply and short-term interest rates.
- **Discount Rate**: The central bank sets the discount rate at which financial institutions can borrow funds, impacting the cost of borrowing and lending in the broader financial system.
- **Reserve Requirements**: Central banks establish reserve requirements that commercial banks must hold, affecting the amount of lending and money creation in the economy.
- **Forward Guidance**: Central banks communicate their future policy intentions to influence market expectations.
- **Quantitative Easing**: Central banks purchase long-term securities to reduce long-term interest rates and stimulate economic activity.

2. Interest Rate Derivatives as Policy Tools

Interest rate derivatives serve as a vital tool for central banks to achieve their monetary policy objectives:

- **Interest Rate Swaps**: Central banks use interest rate swaps to influence the yield curve. By conducting swaps, they can adjust the balance between fixed and floating-rate instruments in the market, affecting the overall level of interest rates.
- **Interest Rate Futures**: Central banks may employ interest rate futures contracts to signal their policy intentions. For example, a central bank can enter into interest rate futures contracts to convey its commitment to maintaining low short-term interest rates.
- **Options and Caps/Floors**: These derivatives allow central banks to hedge or adjust their exposure to interest rate risk. Options and caps/floors provide flexibility in managing the impact of unexpected rate changes.

3. Forward Guidance and Market Expectations

Central banks often use forward guidance, a form of communication, to influence market expectations and guide interest rate movements. Interest rate derivatives play a crucial role in shaping these expectations. Traders and investors closely monitor central bank statements and actions related to derivatives to gauge future policy decisions. For example, if a central bank enters into interest rate swaps that suggest lower future rates, market participants may adjust their positions accordingly, anticipating a more accommodative monetary policy.

4. Impact on Financial Markets

The central bank's use of interest rate derivatives can have a profound impact on financial markets:

- **Yield Curve Manipulation**: Interest rate swaps can be used to flatten or steepen the yield curve, influencing long-term and short-term rates. This, in turn, affects the pricing and performance of various financial instruments.

- **Volatility and Liquidity**: The central bank's activities in the interest rate derivatives market can influence market volatility and liquidity conditions. Traders and investors closely monitor central bank actions for signals about market stability.
- **Market Sentiment**: Central bank interventions in interest rate derivatives can shape market sentiment and influence investor behavior. Expectations about central bank policy can lead to shifts in portfolio allocations and trading strategies.

5. Challenges and Considerations

While interest rate derivatives are powerful tools for central banks, their use also poses challenges:

- **Market Distortion**: Excessive central bank intervention in interest rate derivatives can distort market signals and discourage market-driven price discovery.
- **Counterparty Risk**: Central banks must carefully manage counterparty risk when engaging in derivative transactions, as large positions can expose them to significant credit risk.

Chapter 8: Credit Derivatives

Understanding Credit Default Swaps (CDS)

Credit Default Swaps (CDS) are a class of credit derivatives that have gained significant prominence in financial markets. These instruments are designed to provide protection against credit risk, allowing market participants to hedge or speculate on the creditworthiness of various entities. In this section, we will delve into the mechanics, applications, and implications of Credit Default Swaps (CDS).

1. The Basics of Credit Default Swaps (CDS)

A Credit Default Swap is a financial contract between two parties, typically referred to as the "protection buyer" and the "protection seller." The core purpose of a CDS is to transfer the credit risk associated with a specific reference entity or asset from the protection buyer to the protection seller.

Key Components of a CDS:

- **Reference Entity**: This is the entity or asset whose credit risk is being transferred. It can be a corporation, a sovereign government, or even a structured financial product like a mortgage-backed security.
- **Notional Amount**: The notional amount represents the total principal or face value of the reference entity's debt that is being protected by the CDS. It does not involve an actual exchange of principal.
- **Premium**: The protection buyer pays a premium to the protection seller at regular intervals, typically quarterly. This premium is similar to an insurance premium and compensates the protection seller for taking on the credit risk.
- **Credit Event**: A CDS contract specifies what constitutes a credit event. Common credit events include bankruptcy, default, restructuring, or failure to make interest or principal payments on the reference entity's debt.

- **Payout**: In the event of a credit event, the protection seller is obligated to make a payment to the protection buyer. This payment is usually equal to the difference between the notional amount and the recovery value of the reference entity's debt.

2. Mechanics of Credit Default Swaps (CDS)

The process of a Credit Default Swap unfolds as follows:

- **Contract Initiation**: The protection buyer and protection seller enter into a CDS contract, specifying the reference entity, notional amount, premium, and credit events that trigger a payout.
- **Payment of Premiums**: The protection buyer pays periodic premiums to the protection seller over the life of the contract.
- **Monitoring for Credit Events**: Throughout the contract's term, both parties monitor the creditworthiness of the reference entity. If a specified credit event occurs, the protection buyer can notify the protection seller to trigger the CDS contract.
- **Payout**: In the event of a credit event, the protection seller is obligated to pay the protection buyer an amount determined by the CDS contract terms. This payout is meant to compensate the protection buyer for losses resulting from the credit event.
- **Expiration or Termination**: The CDS contract typically has a specified maturity date, after which it expires. It can also be terminated early if both parties agree to do so.

3. Purposes and Applications of Credit Default Swaps (CDS)

Credit Default Swaps serve various purposes and are used in different financial scenarios:

- **Hedging Credit Risk**: Investors and financial institutions use CDS to hedge against the credit risk associated with their investments in bonds or other credit-sensitive assets. By buying CDS protection, they can offset potential losses from credit events.

- **Speculation**: Traders and investors often use CDS to speculate on the creditworthiness of entities or sectors. For example, they may buy CDS protection on a reference entity if they believe its credit quality is deteriorating.
- **Credit Risk Management**: Banks and financial institutions use CDS to manage their credit exposure to borrowers or counterparties. They may buy CDS protection to reduce their credit risk exposure.
- **Portfolio Diversification**: CDS can be used to diversify portfolios by gaining exposure to specific credit markets or sectors without holding the underlying bonds.

4. Market Implications and Challenges

CDS markets have grown significantly over the years and have faced various challenges and criticisms. Some key considerations include:

- **Liquidity**: CDS markets can experience liquidity fluctuations, especially for less widely traded reference entities. During times of financial stress, liquidity can dry up, making it challenging to enter or exit positions.
- **Counterparty Risk**: CDS contracts involve counterparty risk, as protection sellers are obligated to make payments in the event of a credit event. The financial health of the protection seller is critical in determining the effectiveness of the protection.
- **Regulatory Oversight**: Due to their role in the 2008 financial crisis, CDS markets have undergone regulatory reforms aimed at increasing transparency and reducing systemic risk.

Pricing and Valuation of Credit Default Swaps (CDS)

Credit Default Swaps (CDS) are essential instruments for managing and transferring credit risk in financial markets. To effectively use CDS, market participants need to understand how they are priced and valued. In this section, we will explore the mechanics of pricing and valuing Credit Default Swaps.

1. CDS Pricing Basics

The pricing of a Credit Default Swap involves determining the fair value of the protection provided by the seller to the buyer. Key components in pricing a CDS include:

- **Notional Amount**: The notional amount represents the nominal value of the reference entity's debt being protected by the CDS. It is not exchanged but serves as the basis for calculating the CDS premium and potential payout.
- **Premium**: The premium is the periodic payment made by the protection buyer to the protection seller. It compensates the seller for taking on credit risk. CDS premiums are typically quoted as a spread over a reference interest rate, such as the London Interbank Offered Rate (LIBOR).
- **Credit Spread**: The credit spread is the additional yield above the risk-free rate that an investor receives for holding the reference entity's debt. It is a measure of the reference entity's credit risk. The CDS premium represents this credit spread.

2. Factors Affecting CDS Pricing

Several factors influence the pricing of a Credit Default Swap:

- **Credit Risk of the Reference Entity**: The credit quality of the reference entity is a primary driver of CDS pricing. Entities with higher credit risk will have higher CDS spreads, resulting in larger premiums.
- **Term to Maturity**: The time remaining until the CDS contract's maturity affects the premium. Longer-term CDS contracts typically have higher premiums due to the increased exposure to credit risk over time.
- **Market Sentiment**: Current market conditions and sentiment can impact CDS pricing. In times of market stress or economic uncertainty, CDS spreads may widen, leading to higher premiums.

- **Liquidity of the CDS Market**: Liquidity in the CDS market can affect pricing. More liquid CDS contracts tend to have tighter spreads and lower premiums.

3. Valuation of Credit Default Swaps

Valuation of CDS involves determining the fair market value of an existing contract. Two primary approaches are commonly used:

- **Market Approach**: Under the market approach, CDS contracts are valued based on observable market prices. This approach is straightforward when actively traded CDS contracts exist for the same reference entity and maturity. Market prices provide a transparent valuation.
- **Model Approach**: When market prices are not readily available or when valuing customized or illiquid CDS contracts, mathematical models are used. The most common model used for CDS valuation is the reduced-form model, which considers the probability of default of the reference entity, recovery rates, and the CDS spread to estimate the CDS premium and value.

4. Valuation Challenges

Valuing CDS contracts can be challenging due to several factors:

- **Lack of Market Data**: The availability of market prices for specific CDS contracts can be limited, especially for less liquid reference entities.
- **Counterparty Risk**: CDS valuation must account for counterparty risk. The creditworthiness of the protection seller affects the potential payout in case of a credit event.
- **Model Assumptions**: Valuation models rely on certain assumptions about default probabilities, recovery rates, and market conditions. Changes in these assumptions can impact the valuation.

5. Applications of CDS Valuation

Understanding CDS valuation is crucial for various market participants:

- **Investors**: Investors use CDS valuation to assess the credit risk and potential returns of CDS contracts they hold or consider purchasing.
- **Banks and Financial Institutions**: Banks use CDS valuation to manage their credit risk exposure, assess the creditworthiness of counterparties, and set pricing for CDS products they offer to clients.
- **Regulators**: Regulators may use CDS valuation as part of their oversight of financial institutions to ensure adequate risk management and capital adequacy.

Credit Spread Options

Credit Spread Options are derivative contracts that provide investors with a means to hedge or speculate on changes in credit spreads. These options allow market participants to gain exposure to the credit risk associated with a reference entity or a credit index without directly owning the underlying debt. In this section, we will delve into the mechanics, applications, and implications of Credit Spread Options.

1. Understanding Credit Spread Options

Credit Spread Options are a type of financial contract that derives its value from changes in credit spreads—the yield differential between corporate or sovereign bonds and risk-free government bonds. These options are typically cash-settled and are used to hedge or speculate on movements in credit spreads.

Key Components of Credit Spread Options:

- **Underlying Reference**: Credit Spread Options are linked to an underlying reference entity or credit index. This reference represents the credit risk being traded.
- **Strike Spread**: The strike spread is the predetermined level at which the option will settle. If the actual credit spread at expiration is wider

(higher) than the strike spread for a call option, the option holder receives a payout.

- **Call and Put Options**: Credit Spread Options can be either call options or put options. Call options profit when credit spreads widen, while put options profit when spreads narrow.
- **Expiration Date**: Like other options, Credit Spread Options have an expiration date, after which they cease to have value.

2. Mechanics of Credit Spread Options

The mechanics of Credit Spread Options involve the following steps:

- **Contract Initiation**: A trader or investor purchases a Credit Spread Option linked to a specific reference entity or credit index. The option can be a call or put option.
- **Premium Payment**: The buyer pays a premium to the seller of the option. This premium represents the cost of the option contract and can vary based on market conditions, the credit quality of the reference entity, and other factors.
- **Monitoring Credit Spreads**: Throughout the life of the option, both parties monitor the credit spreads associated with the reference entity or index. Credit spread data is widely available and can be tracked in real-time.
- **Expiration and Settlement**: When the option reaches its expiration date, its value is determined based on the difference between the actual credit spread at that time and the strike spread. Depending on whether it's a call or put option, the option holder may receive a payout.

3. Purposes and Applications of Credit Spread Options

Credit Spread Options serve several purposes in financial markets:

- **Hedging Credit Risk**: Investors can use Credit Spread Options to hedge against credit risk associated with their bond portfolios. For example, a portfolio manager holding corporate bonds can purchase put options to protect against widening credit spreads that may erode the value of the bonds.

- **Speculation**: Traders and investors can speculate on changes in credit spreads by buying call or put options. If they anticipate that credit spreads will widen (narrow), they would purchase call (put) options to profit from the movement.
- **Portfolio Diversification**: Credit Spread Options offer an alternative way to gain exposure to credit risk without directly holding bonds. This can help diversify investment portfolios.

4. Market Implications and Challenges

Credit Spread Options can have implications for financial markets:

- **Liquidity**: Liquidity in Credit Spread Options markets can vary based on the reference entity or index. Options linked to widely tracked references are typically more liquid than those tied to less-known entities.
- **Risk Management**: Credit Spread Options introduce an additional layer of risk management to credit portfolios. However, like any derivative, they also introduce counterparty risk, as the options depend on the financial health of the option counterparties.

Using Credit Derivatives for Credit Risk Management

Credit derivatives are powerful tools that offer a range of strategies for managing and mitigating credit risk. They provide flexibility to investors, institutions, and corporations to tailor their exposure to credit risk according to their specific needs and risk tolerance. In this section, we will explore how credit derivatives are employed for credit risk management.

1. Understanding Credit Risk

Credit risk, also known as default risk, is the risk that a borrower or issuer of debt instruments will fail to meet its financial obligations, such as making interest or principal payments. Credit risk can arise in various financial transactions, including lending, investing in corporate bonds, and holding mortgage-backed securities.

2. The Role of Credit Derivatives

Credit derivatives offer several ways to manage credit risk:

- **Hedging**: Investors and financial institutions can use credit derivatives to hedge their credit exposures. For example, if an investor holds a portfolio of corporate bonds, they can purchase credit default swaps (CDS) to protect against the risk of default by the issuers of those bonds.
- **Credit Enhancement**: Credit derivatives can enhance the credit quality of a bond or loan. Credit enhancement involves using credit derivatives to create a buffer against potential credit losses, making the instrument more appealing to investors.
- **Portfolio Diversification**: Credit derivatives allow investors to gain exposure to a broad range of credit risks without directly holding individual bonds. This diversification can help spread and manage credit risk across a portfolio.

3. Hedging Credit Risk with Credit Default Swaps (CDS)

Credit Default Swaps are one of the most commonly used credit derivatives for hedging credit risk. Here's how they work for credit risk management:

- **Protection Buyer**: The protection buyer is typically an investor or institution that seeks to hedge its exposure to the credit risk of a specific entity or portfolio of assets.
- **Protection Seller**: The protection seller is often a financial institution willing to assume the credit risk in exchange for a premium.
- **Contract Terms**: The CDS contract specifies the reference entity, notional amount, premium payments, and credit events that trigger a

payout.

- **Hedging Scenario**: Suppose an investor holds bonds issued by Company XYZ and is concerned about the company's creditworthiness. The investor can enter into a CDS contract with a protection seller where, in exchange for a premium, the protection seller agrees to compensate the investor in case Company XYZ defaults on its debt.
- **Payout in Case of Default**: If Company XYZ defaults, the protection seller pays the investor an amount equivalent to the loss incurred due to the default. This helps the investor hedge against potential credit losses.

4. Advanced Strategies in Credit Risk Management

Advanced credit risk management strategies using credit derivatives include:

- **Tranche Trading**: Tranche trading involves the buying and selling of different tranches (slices) of credit-linked securities. Investors can tailor their exposure to specific portions of credit risk, allowing for more precise risk management.
- **Structured Credit Products**: Structured credit products combine various credit derivatives to create customized credit risk exposure. These products can be used for risk transfer, credit enhancement, or credit arbitrage.
- **Credit Risk Transfer (CRT)**: CRT programs enable financial institutions to transfer credit risk from their balance sheets to external investors through the issuance of credit-linked notes or securities.

5. Challenges and Considerations

While credit derivatives offer powerful tools for credit risk management, they are not without challenges and considerations:

- **Counterparty Risk**: Credit derivatives involve counterparty risk, as the effectiveness of the hedge depends on the creditworthiness of the protection seller.

- **Regulatory Environment**: The use of credit derivatives is subject to regulatory oversight to ensure transparency, market stability, and risk mitigation.
- **Data and Valuation**: Valuing credit derivatives accurately can be complex, especially for customized products or less liquid reference entities.

Challenges and Controversies in the Credit Derivatives Market

The credit derivatives market has grown significantly over the years, providing valuable tools for managing credit risk. However, like any financial market, it has faced challenges and controversies that have raised concerns among market participants, regulators, and the broader financial community. In this section, we will explore some of the key challenges and controversies associated with the credit derivatives market.

1. Lack of Transparency

One of the persistent challenges in the credit derivatives market has been a lack of transparency. This lack of transparency has several facets:

- **Opaque Pricing**: Pricing of certain credit derivatives, especially customized or complex products, can be opaque. Market participants may struggle to determine fair values, which can lead to mispricing and uncertainty.
- **Counterparty Risk**: Assessing the creditworthiness of counterparties in bilateral credit derivative transactions can be challenging. The 2008 financial crisis highlighted the risks associated with counterparty defaults.
- **Data Reporting**: Accurate and timely reporting of credit derivative transactions has historically been limited, making it difficult for regulators and market participants to monitor market activity effectively.

2. Counterparty Risk

Credit derivatives inherently involve counterparty risk—the risk that the protection seller may default on their obligations in the event of a credit event. The magnitude of this risk became evident during the financial crisis when a series of high-profile counterparty defaults occurred.

To address this issue, central clearing counterparties (CCPs) have been introduced in some credit derivatives markets to act as intermediaries, reducing counterparty risk. However, the transition to CCP clearing has not been without challenges, including concerns about concentration risk and the impact on smaller market participants.

3. Complexity and Customization

Credit derivatives come in a wide variety of structures, including credit default swaps (CDS), collateralized debt obligations (CDOs), and bespoke structured products. The complexity and customization of these instruments can pose challenges:

- **Risk Assessment**: Assessing the risk associated with complex credit derivatives can be difficult, as they often involve multiple layers of exposure to different credit events.
- **Lack of Standardization**: The lack of standardization in certain credit derivatives makes it challenging to compare and assess the risk associated with different products.

4. Regulatory and Legal Issues

The credit derivatives market has faced scrutiny and regulatory changes, particularly in the aftermath of the 2008 financial crisis. Some of the key regulatory and legal issues include:

- **Dodd-Frank Act**: The Dodd-Frank Wall Street Reform and Consumer Protection Act introduced regulations aimed at improving transparency, reducing systemic risk, and enhancing oversight of the derivatives market, including credit derivatives.

- **ISDA Master Agreements**: The International Swaps and Derivatives Association (ISDA) master agreements govern many credit derivative transactions. These agreements have been subject to legal disputes and controversies, particularly during times of market stress.

5. Impact on Financial Crises

The credit derivatives market played a role in the 2008 financial crisis, with the collapse of Lehman Brothers and the subsequent cascade of credit events triggering a wave of credit default swaps. This raised questions about the potential for credit derivatives to exacerbate financial crises.

6. Risk Management Challenges

While credit derivatives offer tools for managing credit risk, they can also pose risk management challenges:

- **Overreliance**: Some market participants may rely too heavily on credit derivatives for risk management, potentially underestimating the complexity and risks involved.
- **Hedging Mismatches**: Misalignments between the risk being hedged and the structure of the credit derivative can result in ineffective risk management.

Chapter 9: Commodity Derivatives

Commodities and Their Role in Derivatives Markets

Commodities have been a fundamental part of human civilization for centuries, serving as essential resources for sustenance, trade, and industrialization. In the context of derivatives markets, commodities hold a unique and crucial role. In this section, we will explore the significance of commodities and their pivotal role in derivatives markets.

1. Understanding Commodities

Commodities are raw materials or primary agricultural products that can be bought and sold, such as agricultural goods (wheat, coffee, soybeans), natural resources (crude oil, natural gas, metals), and even financial instruments like foreign currencies. These tangible assets are essential for daily life, industrial production, and economic development.

2. Historical Significance

Commodities have a rich historical significance:

- **Trade and Civilization**: The exchange of commodities drove early trade and contributed to the rise of civilizations. Spices, textiles, and precious metals were among the first commodities traded across regions.
- **Industrial Revolution**: The Industrial Revolution transformed the demand for commodities as they became vital inputs for manufacturing, infrastructure development, and energy production.
- **Globalization**: Commodities played a central role in globalization, connecting distant parts of the world through trade routes and transportation networks.

3. Commodities in Derivatives Markets

Commodities have a profound influence on derivatives markets for several reasons:

- **Risk Management**: Commodities are subject to price volatility due to factors such as weather conditions, geopolitical events, and supply-demand dynamics. This volatility creates risk for producers, consumers, and traders. Derivatives allow market participants to manage and hedge these price risks.
- **Price Discovery**: Derivatives markets provide valuable information about commodity prices and future expectations. The pricing mechanisms in these markets help determine benchmark prices for commodities worldwide.
- **Speculation**: Speculators participate in commodity derivatives markets to profit from price movements. Their activities contribute to market liquidity and price efficiency.
- **Investment**: Commodity derivatives provide an asset class for investors looking to diversify their portfolios. Investments in commodities can serve as a hedge against inflation and currency fluctuations.

4. Types of Commodity Derivatives

Commodity derivatives encompass a variety of instruments:

- **Futures Contracts**: Futures contracts are agreements to buy or sell a specified quantity of a commodity at a predetermined price on a future date. They are widely used for hedging and speculation.
- **Options Contracts**: Options give the holder the right, but not the obligation, to buy (call option) or sell (put option) a commodity at a predetermined price within a specified period. Options are versatile tools for risk management and trading strategies.
- **Swaps**: Commodity swaps involve exchanging cash flows based on commodity price movements. They can be used for hedging, arbitrage, or portfolio diversification.

5. Role in the Global Economy

Commodities play a vital role in the global economy:

- **Agriculture**: Agricultural commodities are essential for food production and security. Derivatives markets help farmers manage production risks.
- **Energy**: Crude oil and natural gas are crucial energy sources. Energy derivatives markets impact global energy prices and supply chains.
- **Metals**: Metals like copper and aluminum are essential for construction and manufacturing industries. Metals derivatives affect infrastructure development and industrial output.
- **Financial Markets**: Even financial commodities like currencies and interest rates influence monetary policies and international trade.

6. Environmental and Ethical Considerations

The production and trading of commodities have raised concerns about environmental sustainability and ethical practices. Climate change, deforestation, and labor rights are some of the issues that have gained attention in commodity supply chains. As a result, there is growing interest in sustainable and ethical investing in commodities.

Agricultural vs. Energy vs. Metal Derivatives

Commodity derivatives markets are diverse and encompass a wide range of underlying assets. Among the various categories of commodities, agricultural, energy, and metal derivatives are prominent. In this section, we will explore the characteristics, market dynamics, and unique aspects of these three major categories of commodity derivatives.

1. Agricultural Derivatives

a. Characteristics:

Agricultural derivatives are financial instruments tied to the prices of agricultural products. They serve several key functions:

- **Risk Management**: Farmers use agricultural derivatives to manage price risks associated with their crops. For example, a wheat farmer may use a futures contract to lock in a price for their harvest months in advance, reducing uncertainty.
- **Price Discovery**: These derivatives play a vital role in price discovery, establishing benchmarks for the prices of agricultural commodities worldwide. These benchmarks influence both physical and derivative markets.
- **Global Impact**: Agricultural derivatives impact global food prices, food security, and supply chains. Fluctuations in agricultural prices can affect consumers, producers, and policymakers worldwide.

b. Types of Agricultural Derivatives:

- **Grains**: Corn, wheat, and soybeans are among the most actively traded agricultural derivatives. Futures and options contracts on these commodities are popular for hedging and speculation.
- **Soft Commodities**: Soft commodities include coffee, cocoa, sugar, and cotton. They are integral to the global food and beverage industry, and derivatives markets for these commodities offer risk management tools for various stakeholders.
- **Livestock**: Livestock derivatives cover cattle and hogs. These contracts help livestock producers hedge against price volatility in feed and meat prices.

2. Energy Derivatives

a. Characteristics:

Energy derivatives are tied to the prices of energy resources such as crude oil, natural gas, and electricity. They play a pivotal role in the global energy sector and have a broad impact on economies and financial markets:

- **Energy Supply and Demand**: Energy derivatives markets reflect shifts in global supply and demand for energy resources, impacting energy security and geopolitical considerations.

- **Price Volatility**: Energy markets are known for their price volatility, influenced by factors such as geopolitical events, weather patterns, and technological advancements. Energy derivatives help market participants manage these risks.
- **Investment Vehicles**: Energy derivatives offer investors a way to gain exposure to the energy sector without owning physical assets, making them a significant part of investment portfolios.

b. Types of Energy Derivatives:

- **Crude Oil**: Crude oil futures and options are among the most traded derivatives globally. They are used by oil producers, refiners, and traders for hedging and speculation.
- **Natural Gas**: Natural gas derivatives play a vital role in managing price risk for natural gas producers, utilities, and industrial consumers.
- **Electricity**: Electricity derivatives, including futures and options, allow market participants to manage the price risk associated with electricity production and consumption.

3. Metal Derivatives

a. Characteristics:

Metal derivatives are linked to the prices of various metals, including precious metals like gold and silver and industrial metals like copper and aluminum:

- **Industrial Applications**: Industrial metals are essential for manufacturing and construction, making their derivatives important for industries that rely on these materials.
- **Safe Havens**: Precious metals like gold are often seen as safe-haven assets in times of economic uncertainty, influencing investment strategies and portfolios.
- **Global Trade**: Metal derivatives markets impact global trade and

supply chains, as metals are traded worldwide for various applications.

b. Types of Metal Derivatives:

- **Gold and Silver**: Precious metals like gold and silver have a long history as stores of value. Derivatives linked to these metals are used for investment and risk management.
- **Copper**: Copper is a key industrial metal used in construction and manufacturing. Copper derivatives help market participants manage exposure to fluctuations in copper prices.
- **Aluminum**: Aluminum is widely used in the aerospace and automotive industries. Derivatives on aluminum prices are valuable for companies in these sectors.

Pricing and Valuation of Commodity Derivatives

Pricing and valuing commodity derivatives are essential aspects of participating in these markets. Whether you are a producer looking to hedge against price volatility or a trader seeking profit opportunities, understanding how commodity derivatives are priced and valued is crucial. In this section, we will delve into the mechanics and methodologies for pricing and valuing commodity derivatives.

1. Pricing Basics

Pricing commodity derivatives involves determining their fair market value based on various factors:

- **Underlying Commodity**: The price of the underlying commodity is a primary driver of the derivative's value. Factors such as supply and demand, production costs, geopolitical events, and weather conditions can influence commodity prices.
- **Time to Maturity**: The time remaining until the derivative's expiration date affects its value. Generally, the longer the time to maturity, the more uncertainty exists, which can impact the

derivative's price.

- **Interest Rates**: Interest rates can influence the pricing of commodity derivatives, particularly for futures and options contracts. The opportunity cost of tying up capital in a derivative can affect its value.
- **Dividends and Yield**: For commodities that generate income, such as dividend-paying stocks or interest-bearing securities, the income generated can affect the derivative's price.

2. Valuation Methods

Several valuation methods are used for commodity derivatives:

- **Market Approach**: This approach relies on observable market prices. For standardized commodity derivatives, market prices are readily available and are used as the basis for valuation. For example, the closing price of a futures contract on a commodity serves as its daily mark-to-market value.
- **Model Approach**: When market prices are not available or when valuing complex or customized derivatives, mathematical models are employed. The Black-Scholes model, commonly used for options, can be adapted for commodity options. For more complex derivatives, Monte Carlo simulations may be used to estimate their value.

3. Factors Affecting Commodity Derivative Prices

The prices of commodity derivatives are influenced by various factors:

- **Supply and Demand**: Changes in the supply and demand for the underlying commodity can have a direct impact on derivative prices. For example, a drought affecting crop production can lead to higher prices for agricultural commodity derivatives.
- **Volatility**: The level of price volatility in the underlying commodity market can affect the prices of options and other derivatives. Higher volatility generally leads to higher option premiums.
- **Storage Costs**: For physical commodities like oil and metals, storage

costs play a role in pricing. Storage costs can impact the price of futures contracts.

4. Types of Commodity Derivatives Pricing

Different types of commodity derivatives are priced using specific methodologies:

- **Futures Contracts**: The pricing of futures contracts typically relies on the spot price of the underlying commodity and includes adjustments for factors such as interest rates and dividend yields.
- **Options Contracts**: Options pricing involves estimating the expected future value of the option based on factors like the current underlying commodity price, time to expiration, implied volatility, and the option's strike price.

5. Challenges in Pricing and Valuation

Pricing and valuing commodity derivatives can be challenging due to several factors:

- **Illiquidity**: Some commodities and derivative contracts may lack liquidity, making it difficult to determine fair market values.
- **Complexity**: Customized or structured commodity derivatives can be highly complex, requiring sophisticated models and data inputs for valuation.
- **Market Shocks**: Unexpected events, such as natural disasters or geopolitical crises, can disrupt commodity markets and affect pricing models.

Commodity Hedging Strategies for Producers and Consumers

Commodity hedging is a crucial risk management tool for both producers and consumers of commodities. Producers aim to protect themselves from price volatility that can impact their revenues, while consumers seek to mitigate the risk of higher input costs. In this section, we will explore various commodity hedging strategies employed by producers and consumers.

1. For Producers

a. Futures Contracts:

Producers can use futures contracts to lock in prices for their future production. For example, a wheat farmer can sell wheat futures contracts to guarantee a predetermined price for their crop when it's ready for harvest. This hedges against the risk of falling wheat prices.

b. Options Contracts:

Options provide producers with flexibility. A producer can buy put options to establish a price floor for their product while still benefiting from price increases. This allows them to participate in favorable price movements while having downside protection.

c. Forward Contracts:

Forward contracts are customized agreements between two parties, allowing producers to negotiate specific terms that suit their needs. They can tailor the contract's quantity and delivery date to match their production schedule.

d. Basis Hedging:

Basis represents the difference between the local cash price and the futures price for a commodity. Producers can hedge basis risk by selling futures contracts while holding onto their physical commodity. This strategy helps ensure a fixed price, regardless of local price fluctuations.

e. Seasonal Hedging:

Some commodities have seasonal price patterns due to factors like weather or harvest cycles. Producers can use seasonal hedging to lock in prices during peak price periods and deliver their product when prices are favorable.

2. For Consumers

a. Futures Contracts:

Consumers, such as manufacturers or utilities, can use futures contracts to lock in prices for raw materials or energy resources. For instance, an airline may use crude oil futures to hedge against rising fuel costs.

b. Options Contracts:

Consumers can use options to manage price risk while maintaining flexibility. By purchasing call options, they can secure the right to buy commodities at predetermined prices, protecting against price spikes.

c. Physical Forward Contracts:

Consumers can enter into forward contracts to secure a specific price and quantity of a commodity, ensuring a stable cost structure for their operations.

d. Inventory Management:

Some consumers manage their price risk by maintaining strategic inventories of key commodities. This allows them to absorb short-term price fluctuations without impacting their operations.

3. Challenges and Considerations

Both producers and consumers face challenges when implementing commodity hedging strategies:

- **Basis Risk**: Even with hedging, basis risk exists. Factors like transportation costs and local supply and demand can affect the actual price received or paid.
- **Market Liquidity**: Liquidity can vary in commodity derivatives markets, impacting the ease of executing hedging strategies.
- **Margin Requirements**: Both producers and consumers need to consider margin requirements when using futures and options contracts, as they tie up capital.
- **Regulatory Compliance**: Compliance with regulations, including position limits and reporting requirements, is essential for effective

hedging.

Environmental and Ethical Considerations in Commodity Derivatives

Commodity derivatives play a significant role in global financial markets, impacting the pricing and risk management of essential goods and resources. However, the extraction, production, and distribution of commodities can have profound environmental and ethical implications. In this section, we will explore the environmental and ethical considerations associated with commodity derivatives.

1. Environmental Considerations

a. Resource Depletion:

- **Fossil Fuels**: Commodity derivatives linked to fossil fuels, such as crude oil and natural gas, can contribute to resource depletion and environmental degradation. Increased consumption driven by derivatives markets can exacerbate the depletion of finite resources.
- **Metals and Minerals**: The extraction and processing of metals and minerals for industrial use can lead to habitat destruction, water pollution, and soil contamination. Derivatives related to these commodities may indirectly contribute to environmental harm.

b. Climate Change:

- **Carbon Markets**: Derivatives markets related to carbon emissions, like carbon allowances and offsets, are intended to address climate change. However, their effectiveness in reducing greenhouse gas emissions is a subject of debate.
- **Weather Derivatives**: Weather derivatives, used by businesses to hedge against weather-related risks, can indirectly influence climate change mitigation efforts. For example, energy companies might use derivatives to offset revenue losses caused by mild winters, reducing incentives for energy conservation.

c. Agriculture and Land Use:

- **Agricultural Commodities**: Derivatives tied to agricultural commodities can influence land use and deforestation. For instance, high demand for palm oil, driven partly by derivatives, has been linked to deforestation in tropical regions.
- **Water Scarcity**: Agriculture heavily relies on water, and derivatives related to water resources could have implications for water scarcity in certain regions.

2. Ethical Considerations

a. Labor Rights:

- **Supply Chain Ethics**: The production and distribution of commodities often involve complex global supply chains. Ethical concerns arise regarding labor conditions, workers' rights, and fair wages. Derivatives markets can indirectly support industries with questionable labor practices.

b. Food Security:

- **Speculation and Food Prices**: Speculation in commodity derivatives markets, particularly in agricultural commodities, has been linked to food price spikes. These price spikes can have adverse effects on global food security, particularly in vulnerable populations.

c. Conflict Minerals:

- **Metals and Minerals**: Certain metals and minerals, often used in electronics and manufacturing, are sourced from regions with conflict and human rights abuses. Derivatives linked to these commodities can inadvertently support such practices.

3. Mitigation and Responsibility

a. Regulatory Frameworks:

- Governments and international organizations have implemented regulatory frameworks to address some of the environmental and ethical concerns associated with commodity derivatives. For example, regulations may require disclosure of conflict minerals or set limits on speculative positions in futures markets.

b. Responsible Investment:

- Ethical investors and funds may avoid or engage with commodity derivatives based on their environmental and ethical principles. They may prioritize investments in commodities with responsible supply chains and sustainable practices.

c. Corporate Responsibility:

- Companies involved in the production and distribution of commodities have a role in mitigating environmental and ethical concerns. They can adopt responsible sourcing practices, support sustainable agriculture, and invest in cleaner technologies.

Chapter 10: Risk Management and Regulation

The Importance of Risk Management in Derivative Use

Risk management is a foundational principle in the world of finance, and it takes on paramount importance when dealing with derivatives. These sophisticated financial instruments, while offering valuable opportunities for hedging and speculation, also introduce a range of risks that can have profound consequences for individuals, businesses, and the broader financial system. In this section, we will explore the critical role of risk management in derivative use and its significance in safeguarding financial stability.

1. Understanding Risk in Derivative Use

Derivatives, by their very nature, are instruments that derive their value from underlying assets or reference points, such as commodities, interest rates, or stock indices. This inherent link to underlying assets introduces several types of risks:

- **Price Risk**: The most fundamental risk associated with derivatives is price risk, which arises from fluctuations in the value of the underlying asset. Whether you are holding a futures contract, an options contract, or a swap, the value of your position can change rapidly with market movements.
- **Counterparty Risk**: Derivative transactions are often bilateral, meaning they involve two parties entering into an agreement. This introduces counterparty risk, which is the risk that one party may not fulfill its obligations. Counterparty risk became glaringly evident during the 2008 financial crisis when several major institutions faced default.
- **Liquidity Risk**: Some derivatives can be illiquid, meaning there may not be a readily available market to buy or sell them. This lack of liquidity can make it challenging to unwind positions, leading to

significant losses.

- **Credit Risk**: Credit risk is closely tied to counterparty risk. When engaging in derivative transactions, you are essentially extending credit to your counterparty. If the counterparty defaults, you could suffer substantial losses.

2. The Role of Risk Management

Risk management in the context of derivative use is about mitigating and controlling these risks to ensure that they do not lead to catastrophic financial consequences. Effective risk management serves several critical purposes:

- **Protecting Capital**: One of the primary goals of risk management is to protect capital. This means setting limits on the size of positions, establishing stop-loss orders, and having a clear exit strategy in case the market moves against you.
- **Ensuring Business Continuity**: For businesses that use derivatives as part of their operations (such as commodity producers or airlines hedging fuel costs), risk management ensures the continuity of their core business activities, shielding them from financial shocks.
- **Compliance and Regulation**: Regulatory bodies around the world have implemented rules and regulations related to derivative use. Effective risk management is essential for compliance with these regulations, which helps maintain market integrity and stability.

3. Risk Management Tools in Derivatives

Risk management in derivative use involves employing various tools and strategies:

- **Position Sizing**: Determining the appropriate size of a derivative position relative to your overall portfolio is a fundamental risk management technique. This ensures that losses in derivatives do not disproportionately affect your total capital.
- **Stop-Loss Orders**: Traders often use stop-loss orders to limit

potential losses. These are predetermined price levels at which a position will be automatically liquidated if the market moves against it.

- **Diversification**: Spreading your investments across different asset classes and markets can help reduce risk. This principle applies to derivatives as well, where diversifying strategies can involve using multiple types of derivatives or underlying assets.
- **Hedging**: Hedging is a central risk management strategy in derivatives. It involves taking an offsetting position to an existing one, effectively neutralizing or mitigating risk. For instance, a stock investor might use put options to hedge against potential losses.

4. Regulation and Oversight

The importance of risk management in derivatives has led to extensive regulatory frameworks worldwide. These regulations aim to enhance transparency, reduce systemic risk, and protect market participants. Some key aspects of derivative regulation include:

- **Central Clearing**: In the wake of the 2008 financial crisis, central clearing counterparties (CCPs) were established to act as intermediaries in derivative transactions. They guarantee the fulfillment of contract obligations, reducing counterparty risk
- **Margin Requirements**: Regulators often require market participants to post collateral (margin) to cover potential losses. Margin requirements serve as a risk management tool by ensuring that parties have sufficient capital to meet their obligations.
- **Reporting and Transparency**: Derivative transactions are subject to reporting requirements, enabling regulators to monitor market activity and identify potential risks or anomalies.

5. The Future of Risk Management in Derivative Use

As financial markets evolve and technology advances, risk management in derivative use is also evolving. Some trends and developments in the future of risk management include:

- **Technology and Automation**: Artificial intelligence, machine learning, and data analytics are increasingly being employed for risk management in derivatives. These technologies can provide real-time risk assessment and predictive analytics.
- **Sustainability and ESG**: Environmental, social, and governance (ESG) considerations are becoming integral to risk management. Investors and businesses are factoring ESG risks into their derivative strategies.
- **Cybersecurity**: The digitalization of financial markets brings new risks, particularly in terms of cybersecurity. Robust cybersecurity measures are critical for protecting derivative trading systems and data.

Risk Management Frameworks and Strategies

Risk management in the world of derivatives requires more than just a superficial understanding of risk factors. It necessitates the development and implementation of comprehensive frameworks and strategies that can effectively identify, assess, mitigate, and monitor risks. In this section, we will explore the essential components of risk management frameworks and strategies in the context of derivatives.

1. Risk Management Frameworks

Risk management frameworks provide the structure and guidelines for managing risks associated with derivative use. These frameworks typically encompass the following key components:

a. Risk Identification:

- *Risk Categories*: Derivative risks are diverse, including market risk, credit risk, liquidity risk, operational risk, and legal risk. A robust framework begins with the identification of these risk categories.

- *Risk Assessment*: Within each risk category, assess specific risks related to the derivatives you are using. For example, evaluate the market risk associated with changes in underlying asset prices or interest rates.

b. Risk Measurement:

- *Quantitative Analysis*: Use mathematical models and statistical tools to quantify risks. Value at Risk (VaR), stress testing, and scenario analysis are common techniques.
- *Qualitative Analysis*: Complement quantitative measures with qualitative assessments, considering factors that may not be easily quantifiable, such as geopolitical events or market sentiment.

c. Risk Mitigation:

- *Hedging Strategies*: Develop strategies for hedging risks. For example, if you are exposed to foreign exchange risk, implement currency hedging using options or forward contracts.
- *Diversification*: Spread risk across different asset classes or markets to reduce concentration risk.
- *Limit Setting*: Establish risk limits for each risk category, ensuring that exposures remain within predefined tolerances.

d. Risk Monitoring and Reporting:

- *Real-Time Monitoring*: Use technology and systems to monitor risks in real-time. Automated alerts can signal when risk limits are approached or breached.
- *Periodic Reporting*: Generate regular reports summarizing risk exposures, strategies, and performance against risk limits. These reports facilitate informed decision-making.

2. Risk Management Strategies

Once risks are identified and assessed, risk management strategies are implemented to control and mitigate these risks. Some common risk management strategies in the context of derivatives include:

a. Hedging:

- *Purpose*: Hedging is a core risk management strategy in derivatives. It involves taking positions that offset the risk of existing exposures. For instance, a producer might hedge against falling commodity prices with futures contracts.
- *Types*: Depending on the risk, various derivative instruments can be used for hedging, including futures, options, swaps, and forwards.

b. Portfolio Diversification:

- *Purpose*: Diversifying a portfolio of derivatives can reduce overall risk. By spreading investments across different asset classes, industries, or geographic regions, you can reduce the impact of adverse movements in one area.
- *Asset Allocation*: Determine the appropriate mix of assets within your portfolio, considering your risk tolerance and investment goals.

c. Risk-Return Trade-off:

- *Purpose*: Assess the trade-off between risk and return for each derivative investment. High-risk strategies may offer the potential for greater returns but come with higher risks.
- *Risk-Adjusted Returns*: Evaluate investments based on their risk-adjusted returns, considering the amount of risk taken to achieve a given level of return.

d. Stress Testing:

- *Purpose*: Stress tests simulate extreme market scenarios to assess how a derivative portfolio would perform under adverse conditions.

- *Scenario Analysis*: Create hypothetical scenarios, such as market crashes or economic crises, to gauge the impact on the portfolio's value.

3. Evolving Trends in Risk Management

Risk management in the world of derivatives is not static; it evolves in response to changing market dynamics and technological advancements. Some emerging trends in risk management include:

a. Big Data and Analytics:

- *Purpose*: Utilize advanced data analytics and artificial intelligence to process large volumes of data and identify risk patterns and opportunities.

b. Machine Learning Models:

- *Purpose*: Develop machine learning models that can adapt to changing market conditions and improve the accuracy of risk assessments.

c. Environmental, Social, and Governance (ESG) Integration:

- *Purpose*: Integrate ESG factors into risk management frameworks to address ethical and sustainability considerations.

d. Cybersecurity:

- *Purpose*: Enhance cybersecurity measures to protect against cyber threats and data breaches that could compromise risk management systems.

Basel III and Derivatives Regulation

Regulation plays a pivotal role in the world of derivatives, shaping the landscape in which these complex financial instruments are traded and managed. Among the most significant regulatory frameworks that impact the use of derivatives is Basel III. In this section, we will delve into Basel III and its implications for derivatives regulation.

1. Understanding Basel III

Basel III is a set of international banking standards developed by the Basel Committee on Banking Supervision (BCBS), a global forum for banking supervision. It was introduced as a response to the global financial crisis of 2007-2008, with the primary aim of strengthening the resilience of the global banking system. Basel III includes a range of reforms and regulations, many of which have direct implications for derivatives markets.

2. Basel III and Derivatives Regulation

a. Capital Adequacy Requirements:

One of the central tenets of Basel III is the enhancement of capital adequacy requirements for banks. Banks are required to maintain higher levels of capital to absorb losses and withstand financial stress. This has implications for derivatives regulation in several ways:

- **Credit Valuation Adjustment (CVA) Risk**: Basel III introduced capital requirements for CVA risk, which is particularly relevant in derivatives markets. Banks must hold capital against potential losses arising from counterparty default risk.
- **Market Risk**: The revised market risk framework under Basel III impacts banks' trading activities, including derivatives trading. It introduces standardized and internal model-based approaches to calculate capital charges for market risk.

b. Counterparty Credit Risk (CCR):

Basel III focuses on counterparty credit risk, a significant aspect of derivatives regulation. The following aspects are noteworthy:

- **Central Clearing**: Basel III encourages the use of central clearing counterparties (CCPs) for standardized derivatives. CCPs play a crucial role in reducing counterparty risk by acting as intermediaries that guarantee the fulfillment of derivatives contracts.

- **Credit Risk Mitigation**: Basel III allows banks to recognize the use of eligible collateral as a form of credit risk mitigation when engaging in derivatives transactions. This incentivizes collateralization in the derivatives market.

c. Liquidity Risk:

Basel III addresses liquidity risk in the banking sector, which has implications for the derivatives market, especially for over-the-counter (OTC) derivatives:

- **Net Stable Funding Ratio (NSFR)**: Basel III introduces the NSFR, which requires banks to maintain a stable funding profile over the longer term. This may impact banks' ability to provide liquidity in the derivatives market.

d. Regulatory Reporting and Transparency:

Basel III emphasizes transparency and regulatory reporting. This aspect of the framework affects derivatives regulation in the following ways:

- **Trade Reporting**: Regulatory authorities require reporting of derivative transactions to central repositories. This enhances transparency in the market and aids regulators in monitoring systemic risks.
- **Risk Data Aggregation**: Basel III mandates improved risk data aggregation and reporting, which is essential for monitoring risks associated with derivatives portfolios.

e. Margin and Capital for Non-Cleared Derivatives:

Basel III introduced margin requirements for non-centrally cleared derivatives. These requirements are designed to mitigate counterparty risk and promote responsible risk management practices in the OTC derivatives market.

3. Global Implementation and Adaptation

Basel III is not a one-size-fits-all framework, and its implementation can vary from one jurisdiction to another. National regulators have the flexibility to adapt the framework to suit their specific financial systems and conditions. This adaptation process can result in variations in how derivatives regulation is applied across different regions.

4. Evolving Challenges and Future Considerations

As financial markets evolve, Basel III and derivatives regulation face ongoing challenges and considerations:

- **Technological Advancements**: The rapid evolution of technology, including blockchain and distributed ledger technology, may impact derivatives markets and require regulatory adaptation.
- **Sustainability and ESG Integration**: Environmental, social, and governance (ESG) considerations are gaining prominence in financial markets. Integrating ESG factors into derivatives regulation is a growing trend.
- **Cybersecurity**: The digitalization of derivatives markets requires robust cybersecurity measures to protect against cyber threats that could disrupt market integrity.

Dodd-Frank Act and its Impact on Derivatives Markets

The Dodd-Frank Wall Street Reform and Consumer Protection Act, commonly referred to as Dodd-Frank, is a landmark piece of financial legislation enacted in the United States in 2010. This comprehensive law was introduced in response to the global financial crisis of 2007-2008 and aims to enhance financial stability, protect consumers, and reform various aspects of the financial industry. In this section, we will explore the Dodd-Frank Act and its profound impact on derivatives markets.

1. Understanding Dodd-Frank

The Dodd-Frank Act encompasses a wide range of provisions that touch on nearly every aspect of the financial system. However, it is particularly noteworthy for the extensive reforms it introduced to derivatives markets. Key components of Dodd-Frank related to derivatives include:

a. Central Clearing:

Dodd-Frank encourages central clearing of standardized derivatives contracts through central clearing counterparties (CCPs). This provision aims to reduce counterparty risk and enhance transparency in the derivatives market.

b. Swap Execution Facilities (SEFs):

Dodd-Frank mandates the registration and regulation of SEFs, electronic platforms where market participants can execute swaps. SEFs promote transparency and competitive trading in the derivatives market.

c. Reporting and Recordkeeping:

The Act requires swap data reporting and recordkeeping to enhance transparency and provide regulators with valuable data for monitoring systemic risk.

d. Margin and Capital Requirements:

Dodd-Frank introduced margin requirements for non-cleared swaps, reducing counterparty risk in the over-the-counter (OTC) derivatives market. These requirements are designed to ensure that market participants have sufficient collateral to cover potential losses.

e. Position Limits:

The Act grants the Commodity Futures Trading Commission (CFTC) the authority to establish position limits on futures and options contracts. These limits are aimed at preventing excessive speculation and market manipulation.

2. Impact on Derivatives Markets

Dodd-Frank has had a profound impact on derivatives markets, both in the United States and globally:

a. Increased Transparency:

One of the primary objectives of Dodd-Frank was to bring greater transparency to the derivatives market. The introduction of centralized clearing and reporting requirements has made it easier for regulators to monitor market activity and assess systemic risks.

b. Standardization:

To facilitate central clearing and electronic trading, Dodd-Frank promoted the standardization of derivative contracts. This standardization has made derivatives more liquid and accessible.

c. Counterparty Risk Mitigation:

Through margin and capital requirements, Dodd-Frank has significantly reduced counterparty risk in the derivatives market. The use of CCPs for clearing has become more widespread, further enhancing risk mitigation.

d. Market Structure Changes:

The Act's provisions on SEFs and electronic trading have led to shifts in market structure, with a greater emphasis on electronic platforms and competitive pricing.

e. Global Implications:

While Dodd-Frank is a U.S. law, its impact extends beyond U.S. borders. Many global financial institutions and market participants must comply with its provisions when conducting business in U.S. derivatives markets.

3. Challenges and Ongoing Considerations

Despite its positive contributions to derivatives markets, Dodd-Frank has also faced challenges and ongoing considerations:

- **Regulatory Complexity**: The extensive regulatory framework created by Dodd-Frank has been criticized for its complexity and the compliance burden it places on market participants.
- **Cross-Border Implications**: The extraterritorial reach of Dodd-Frank has raised challenges related to the application of its provisions to non-U.S. entities and transactions.

- **Evolving Market Dynamics**: The derivatives market continues to evolve, with new products and technologies emerging. Regulatory authorities must adapt to these changes while maintaining the Act's core objectives.

International Regulatory Harmonization and Future Trends

The world of derivatives operates on a global scale, with financial instruments traversing borders and markets interconnected as never before. To ensure the stability and integrity of these markets, international regulatory harmonization has become a critical consideration. In this section, we will explore the concept of regulatory harmonization and delve into future trends that may shape the derivatives landscape.

1. Regulatory Harmonization in Derivatives

Regulatory harmonization in the context of derivatives refers to the coordination and alignment of rules and regulations across different jurisdictions. The primary goals of harmonization are:

a. Reducing Regulatory Arbitrage:

When regulations in one jurisdiction are significantly different from those in another, market participants may exploit these differences to engage in regulatory arbitrage. This can lead to risks and distortions in the global derivatives market.

b. Enhancing Market Integrity:

Harmonized regulations help maintain market integrity by ensuring consistent standards for trading, clearing, reporting, and risk management. This promotes fairness and transparency in derivatives markets.

c. Mitigating Systemic Risk:

Consistent regulatory frameworks can mitigate systemic risk by reducing the potential for regulatory gaps and ensuring that market participants adhere to robust risk management practices.

2. International Initiatives for Regulatory Harmonization

Several international initiatives and organizations play pivotal roles in advancing regulatory harmonization in derivatives markets:

a. International Organization of Securities Commissions (IOSCO):

IOSCO is a global body that brings together securities regulators from around the world. It has developed principles for the regulation and supervision of derivatives markets to promote consistency and best practices.

b. Committee on Payments and Market Infrastructures (CPMI) and International Organization of Securities Commissions (IOSCO):

CPMI and IOSCO have jointly developed international standards for financial market infrastructures (FMIs), including derivatives clearinghouses. These standards help ensure the robustness and resilience of FMIs.

c. Financial Stability Board (FSB):

The FSB monitors and makes recommendations about the global financial system to promote stability. It has been instrumental in coordinating efforts to enhance the regulation and oversight of derivatives markets.

3. Future Trends in Derivatives Regulation

The landscape of derivatives regulation continues to evolve. Several key trends are likely to shape the future of derivatives markets:

a. ESG Integration:

Environmental, social, and governance (ESG) considerations are becoming integral to derivatives regulation. Regulators are increasingly focusing on the incorporation of ESG factors into risk assessments and disclosures.

b. Technology and Innovation:

Advancements in technology, including blockchain and artificial intelligence, are poised to revolutionize derivatives markets. Regulators will need to adapt to these changes while ensuring that they do not compromise market integrity or introduce new risks.

c. Cybersecurity:

The digitalization of derivatives markets brings increased vulnerability to cyber threats. Regulatory authorities will need to prioritize cybersecurity measures to protect market infrastructure and data.

d. Cross-Border Coordination:

As derivatives markets become more interconnected, the need for cross-border coordination and harmonization becomes more critical. Regulators must work together to address regulatory challenges that arise from cross-border activities.

e. Post-Pandemic Considerations:

The COVID-19 pandemic has highlighted the importance of robust risk management and contingency planning in derivatives markets. Regulators will likely emphasize the need for enhanced resilience and business continuity measures.

4. The Importance of Regulatory Adaptation

Derivatives markets are dynamic, and regulatory frameworks must adapt to changing circumstances. Regulatory authorities must strike a delicate balance between promoting innovation and ensuring market stability. The ability to anticipate and respond to emerging risks and trends will be crucial for effective derivatives regulation in the future.

Conclusion

International regulatory harmonization is essential for maintaining the stability and integrity of global derivatives markets. As derivatives continue to evolve and become more interconnected, regulators must collaborate on common standards and best practices. Future trends, such as ESG integration, technological innovation, and cybersecurity, will shape the regulatory landscape, requiring regulatory authorities to remain vigilant and adaptive in safeguarding the soundness of derivatives markets. Understanding the evolving nature of derivatives regulation and its global implications is vital for market participants, regulators, and policymakers in navigating the complexities of the derivatives landscape.

Plea for Review:

Dear Reader,

We hope that you've embarked on an enlightening journey through the realm of derivatives within the pages of "Unlocking the Power of Derivatives." Our dedication to clarity, understanding, and financial insight has been infused into every aspect of this book, and now we eagerly await your feedback.

Your review is invaluable to us. It not only guides our future work but also helps fellow readers navigate the world of derivatives. Whether you found our explanations illuminating, our examples insightful, or have suggestions for enhancement, we want to hear from you.

Please take a moment to share your thoughts and insights by leaving a review on your preferred platform. Your review not only empowers us but also assists others in their quest to master the art of derivatives.

Thank you for joining us on this educational adventure, and we look forward to your review.

Warm regards,

Alex Thompson

Don't miss out!

Visit the website below and you can sign up to receive emails whenever Alex Thompson publishes a new book. There's no charge and no obligation.

https://books2read.com/r/B-A-FEPY-BLAOC

BOOKS 2 READ

Connecting independent readers to independent writers.

Also by Alex Thompson

Alex on Finance

Financial Freedom Roadmap - Achieving Early Retirement through the FIRE Movement

The Art of Strategic Innovation

Beyond Cash - The Evolution of Digital Payment Systems and the Future of Money

Preserving Wealth in Inflationary Times - Strategies for Protecting Your Financial Future

Standalone

Side Hustle Success: Unlocking Your Entrepreneurial Potential

Side Hustle Success: The Ultimate Guide to Passive and Financial Freedom

Mastering the Markets: Advanced Trading Strategies for Success and Ethical Trading Practices

Financial Fortitude

Mastering the Art of Upselling

The Financial Bullet Blueprint

Investing Demystified: A Beginner's Guide to Building Wealth in the Stock Market

Real Estate Riches: Building Wealth through Property Investment

How To Succeed as a Freelancer

Navigating Complex Waters: Advanced Strategies in Portfolio Management

Behavioral Finance and Investor Psychology

Leading with Empathy: Harnessing Emotional Intelligence for Effective Leadership
Financial Independence
Thriving Within Your Means: A Guide to Affordable Living
Algorithmic Trading: Navigating the Digital Frontier
Navigating Alternative Investments
Navigating the Behavioral Finance Landscape
Unlocking the Power of Derivatives

www.ingramcontent.com/pod-product-compliance
Lightning Source LLC
LaVergne TN
LVHW022057200926
848481LV00003B/959